WORLD HERITAGE in KOREA

이 도서의 국립중앙도서관 출판예정도서목록(CIP)은 서지정보유통지원시스템 홈페이지(http://seoji.nl.go.kr)와 국가자료공동목록시스템(http://www.nl.go.kr/kolisnet)에서 이용하실 수 있습니다.(CIP제어번호: CIP2015019628)

WORLD HERITAGE in KOREA

Initiated by : A&A Culture Institute

Written by : Nam Chang Geun Baek Gil-Nam Sim Joon Yong Lee Jun Sung Lee Ji Eun Lee Hyun Sung Jeoung Myoung Sik Cho Doo Won Jo Eugene

Publisher : Cho Eun Kyoung

Editor : Yi Bu Seob

designer : Park Min Hee

Published by : Nulbom

Registration Number : Je300-1996-106Ho. 8. 8. 1996

address : Dongsung4gil 9, Jongro-gu, Seoul, Korea

Tel : 822-743-7784

Fax : 822-743-7078

1st edition : 15. 8. 2015

ISBN 978-89-6555-038-9 04910 (SET)

ISBN 978-89-6555-040-2 04910 (WORLD HERITAGE in KOREA)

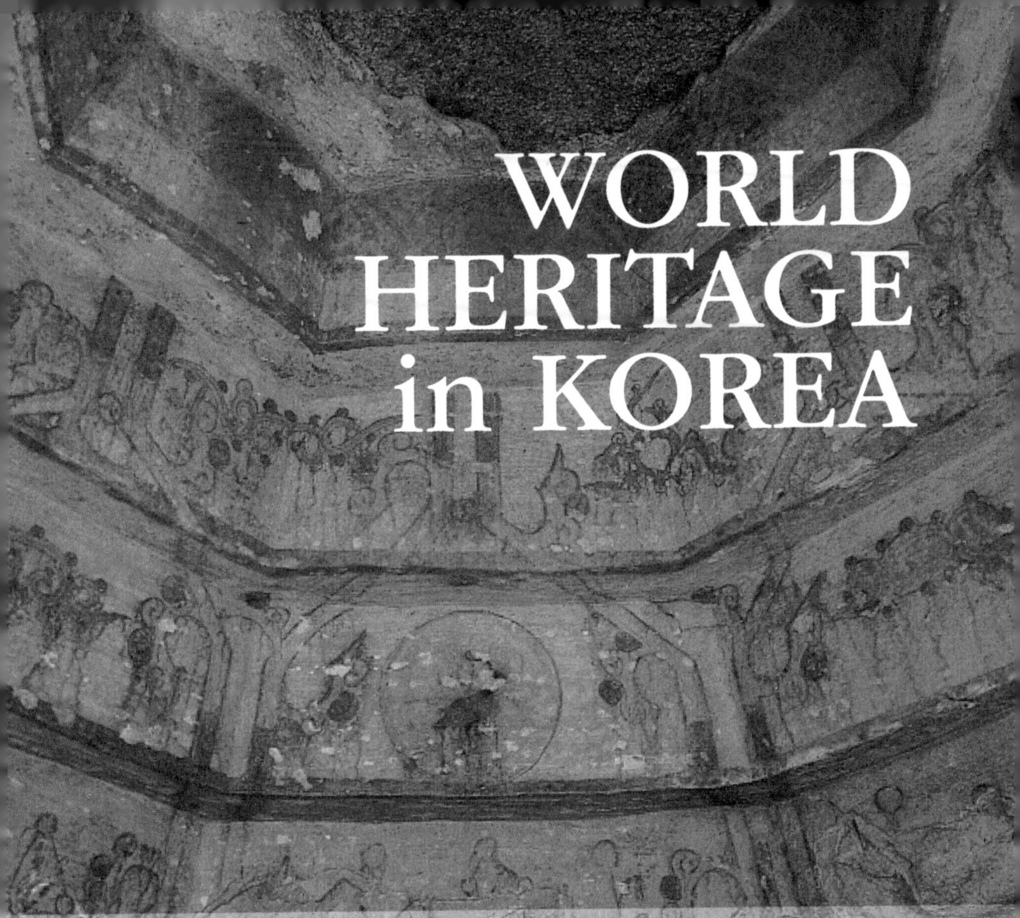

WORLD HERITAGE in KOREA

WRITER Nam C.G. BaeK G.N. Sim J.Y. Lee. J.S. Lee J.E. Lee H.S. Jeoung M.S. Cho D.W. Jo E.G.

Contents

Introduction

This book presents and introduces the 14 World Heritage sites in the Korean Peninsula. The land is currently divided into two Koreas, South and North, which share a history from the prehistoric times to the early 20th century. Diverse types of heritage in the peninsula are enlisted as UNESCO World Heritage, providing glimpses into the important moments of the long history.

There are in fact many other books on the same theme of World Heritage. But books written by those who are actually responsible for the heritage management on site and on the field are rather rare. This book is written by those who are academically dedicated to the field of heritage and who actually work on the projects of nomination, conservation, and management of World Heritage in Korea. The text and photos are the glimpses of their many days in the field.

• **World Heritage** : Jongmyo Shrine(1995), Seokguram Grotto and Bulguksa Temple(1995), Haeinsa Temple Janggyeong Panjeon, Depositories for the Tripitaka Koreana Woodblocks(1995), Hwaseong Fortress(1997), Changdeokgung Palace Complex(1997), Gochang, Hwasun and Ganghwa Dolmen Sites(2000), Gyeongju Historic Areas(2000), Royal Tombs of the Joseon Dynasty(2009), Jeju Volcanic Island and Lava Tubes(2007), Historic Villages of Korea : Hahoe and Yangdong(2010), Namhansanseong(2014), Baekje Historic Areas(2015)

• **Memory of the World** : Archives of SaemaulUndong: New Community Movement(2013), Nanjung Ilgi: War Diary of Admiral Yi Sun-sin(2013), Human Rights Documentary Heritage 1980 Archives for the May 18th Democratic Uprising against Military Regime, in Gwangju, Republic of Korea(2011), Ilseongnok: Records of Daily Reflections(2011), Donguibogam: Principles and Practice of Eastern Medicine(2009), Printing woodblocks of the Tripitaka Koreana and miscellaneous Buddhist scriptures(2007), Uigwe: The Royal Protocols of the Joseon Dynasty(2007), buljojikjisimcheyojeol (vol.II), the second volume of Anthology of Great Buddhist Priests Zen Teachings(2001), Seungjeongwonllgi, the Diaries of the Royal Secretariat(2001), The Annals of the Joseon Dynasty(1997), The HunminChongum Manuscript(1997)

· **Intangile Cultural Heritage** : Nongak, community band music, dance and rituals in the Republic of Korea(2014), Kimjang, making and sharing kimchi in the Republic of Korea(2013), Arirang, lyrical folk song in the Republic of Korea(2012), Falconry, a living human heritage(2012), Jultagi, tightrope walking(2011), Taekkyeon, a traditional Korean martial art(2011), Weaving of Mosi (fine ramie) in the Hansan region(2011), Daemokjang, traditional wooden architecture(2010), Gagok, lyric song cycles accompanied by an orchestra(2010), Cheoyongmu(2009), Ganggangsullae(2009), Jeju Chilmeoridang Yeongdeunggut(2009), NamsadangNori(2009), Yeongsanjae(2009), GangneungDanoje festival(2008), Pansori epic chant(2008), Royal ancestral ritual in the Jongmyo shrine and its music(2008)

It has been the focus of the authors to present the heritage clearly and coherently, to be enjoyable to those who are not familiar with the history and culture of Korea, with the addition of interesting details and features. The book will definitely help in designing a fascinating trip following the World Heritage of Korea.

7. 2015

Nam Chang Geun   Baek Gil-Nam   Sim Joon Yong   Lee Jun Sung   Lee Ji Eun Lee Hyun Sung   Jeoung Myoung Sik   Cho Doo Won   Jo Eugene

What is World Heritage?

Jo Eugene (Konkuk University)

A promise to protect the values

What is needed to become a World Heritage? A site does not qualify for World Heritage merely because it is popular amongst visitors or because it appears grand and exquisite to the eye. Ten criteria are established within the World Heritage Convention which provides guidance to the qualifications. If one or more of the criteria is fulfilled, the heritage is deemed to have values as World Heritage, and the State Party must pledge to protect those values effectively in order to attain the status. In other words, if a heritage does not possess the values outlined in the World Heritage Convention, it cannot be enlisted even if it is globally famous. More over if the State Party does not have the will to protect the heritage, it cannot be enlisted regardless of possessing such values. On the other hand, those heritage which may be virtually unknown to the general public but has intrinsic values and are well supported by the State Party in the protection of its values, can be inscribed on the World Heritage List.

Criteria for Justification of World Heritage

(i) to represent a masterpiece of human creative genius → Seokguram Grotto and Bulguksa Temple

(ii) to exhibit an important interchange of human values, over a span of time or within a cultural area of the world, on developments in architecture or technology, monumental arts, town-planning or landscape design → Changdeokgung Palace Complex, Hwaseong Fortress, Gyeongju Historic Areas, Namhansanseong, Baekje Historic Areas

(iii) to bear a unique or at least exceptional testimony to a cultural tradition or to a civilization which is living or which has disappeared → Changdeokgung Palace Complex, Hwaseong Fortress, Gochang, Hwasun and Ganghwa Dolmen Sites, Gyeongju Historic Areas, Royal Tombs of the Joseon Dynasty, Historic Villages of Korea: Hahoe and Yangdong, Baekje Historic Areas

(iv) to be an outstanding example of a type of building, architectural or technological ensemble or landscape which illustrates (a) significant stage(s) in human history → Jongmyo Shrine, Haeinsa Janggyeong Panjeon, the Depositories for the Tripitaka Koreana Woodblocks, Seokguram Grotto and Bulguksa Temple, Changdeokgung Palace Complex, Royal Tombs of the Joseon Dynasty,

Historic Villages of Korea: Hahoe and Yangdong, Namhansanseong

(v) to be an outstanding example of a traditional human settlement, land-use, or sea-use which is representative of a culture (or cultures), or human interaction with the environment especially when it has become vulnerable under the impact of irreversible change

(vi) to be directly or tangibly associated with events or living traditions, with ideas, or with beliefs, with artistic and literary works of outstanding universal significance. (The Committee considers that this criterion should preferably be used in conjunction with other criteria) → Haeinsa Janggyeong Panjeon, the Depositories for the Tripitaka Koreana Woodblocks, Royal Tombs of the Joseon Dynasty

(vii) to contain superlative natural phenomena or areas of exceptional natural beauty and aesthetic importance → Jeju Volcanic Island and Lava Tubes

(viii) to be outstanding examples representing major stages of earth's history, including the record of life, significant on-going geological processes in the development of landforms, or significant geomorphic or physiographic features → Jeju Volcanic Island and Lava Tubes

(ix) to be outstanding examples representing significant on-going ecological and biological processes in the evolution and development of terrestrial, fresh water, coastal and marine ecosystems and communities of plants and animals

(x) to contain the most important and significant natural habitats for in-situ conservation of biological diversity, including those containing threatened species of outstanding universal value from the point of view of science or conservatio

The status of World Heritage is endowed on those sites which are significant not only to an individual city or country, but to all humanity. If the heritage is considered to have values which can be appreciated and protected by all humanity, it can be enlisted as World Heritage. From then on the duties of protection belongs to the local residents, citizens of the country and people of the world.

Protecting a heritage on the international level might seem a little too grand to grasp the meaning but it is rather simple. It means that from the moment the heritage is enlisted, it has to be protected according to the highest standards of conservation and protection within the country and within the world. UNESCO and other countries have the responsibility to assist and cooperate for the sound protection of the heritage. In other words, the responsibility to protect the heritage becomes a wider, shared commitment amongst the international community. If by any chance the State Party which possesses the heritage is not capable of protecting the heritage, other countries that are part of the Convention must consider it to be their own responsibility to actively protect and hand over the heritage to the future generation.

The World Heritage Convention is an instrument which outlines such responsibilities and duties, together with methods to actually apply them. To protect a heritage according to the highest standards is a grand cause, but without clear and precise implementation methods it would be difficult to achieve such standards. A World Heritage status is not given because the heritage is merely excellent and magnificent. Enlisting a heritage on the list means to pledge for the protection of the heritage. To ensure strong protection, the Outstanding Universal Value of the heritage must be established first and all the stakeholders connected to the heritage must agree with the identified value. Only then can policy decisions on what, when, where, and how to protect the heritage can be made.

Relationship of value and protection

There are three categories in World Heritage. Cultural properties, natural properties and mixed properties which possess both cultural and natural values in the same space. The heritage must all be immovable heritage. Any property that can be removed to a museum or can be transferred from its site cannot become a World Heritage. The heritage also needs to be tangible. Intangible heritage such as actions, knowledge and traditions do not come into the scope of World Heritage. Out of the ten criteria laid out to determine the eligibility of a site, six are cultural criteria and four are natural criteria. Mixed properties must fulfill at least one from both cultural and natural criteria.

The value of a heritage may seem very distant but it plays a very important and practical role when finding ways to protect the heritage. The values of a heritage show the direction of how and what to protect. The values of the Royal Tombs of the Joseon Dynasty which was inscribed as World Heritage in 2009 may serve as an example in portraying this.

According to criterion 3, within the context of Confucian cultures, the integrated approach of the Royal Tombs of Joseon to nature and the universe has resulted in a distinctive and significant funeral tradition. Through the application of pungsu principles and the retention of the natural landscape, a memorable type of sacred place has been created for the practice of ancestral rituals.[1)]

---

1) The Royal Tombs of the Joseon Dynasty was enlisted as World Heritage by justifying criteria (iii), (iv), and (vi).

This text shows what features of the royal tombs must be protected and how. First of all it points out that the surrounding natural landscape and location of the tombs, and the funerary tradition and practice of ancestral rituals are important features of the heritage. These are the objects which need to be protected. Once the object has been identified, the boundaries including these elements can be drawn. The values of the heritage described in words are thus translated into a certain space and/or structures that we can see and touch.

Next it outlines "how" the property must be protected. The Royal Tombs of the Joseon Dynasty are sacred spaces respecting the natural landscape and layout. In other words, the surrounding environment which constitutes the geomantic rationale needs to be protected, and one must not tamper with the original layout which composes the sacredness of the location. All activities or policies which are conducted for the protection of the site have towards the final objective of protecting the environmental surroundings and the sacredness of the tomb space. The establishment of such values of the heritage is also useful in determining the order of priority when there are numerous projects or activities planned at the same time. Projects which better conform to the protection of the Outstanding Universal Value are pursued first.

Jeju Volcanic Island and Lava Tubes is another example. It is the only natural World Heritage in Korea. As is shown in the title, the heritage consists of the volcanic features and underground lava caves in Jeju Island. To be exact the heritage is composed of the Hallasan Mountain, Seongsan Ilchulbong Tuff Cone and the five lava tubes originating from Geomunoreum. It must be noted that the World Heritage does not include the entire island of Jeju.

The volcanic features of Jeju were inscribed on the World Heritage List by fulfilling criteria (vii) and (viii) of the World Heritage Convention. The text describing the justification of criterion (viii) reads as follows. "Jeju has a distinctive value as one of the few large shield volcanoes in the world built over a hot spot on a stationary continental crust plate. It is distinguished by the Geomunoreum lava tube system, which is the most impressive and significant series of protected lava tube caves in the world and includes a spectacular array of secondary carbonate speleothems (stalactites and other decorations), with an abundance and diversity unknown elsewhere within a lava cave. The Seongsan Ilchulbong tuff cone has exceptional exposures of its structural and sedimentological characteristics, making it a world-class location for understanding Surtseyan-type volcanic eruptions." Although it seems slightly long and elaborate, reading it carefully we can understand that Jeju's geological features are composed of the large size shield

World Heritage, Intangible Cultural Heritage and Memory of the World

Currently UNESCO runs three separate programs for enlisting and protecting heritage of the world. These are World Heritage, Intangible Cultural Heritage and Memory of the World programs.

All three programs are different in their scope and method of implementation. World Heritage and Intangible Cultural Heritage are implemented as international conventions with strong legal basis. The Memory of the World is a program initiated by UNESCO implemented with the voluntary participation of States Parties.

As mentioned before World Heritage is limited to those heritage that are tangible and immovable. However as all heritage are embedded with spiritual values a criterion on 'associated values' is also set out.

Intangible Cultural Heritage aims at safeguarding rituals, traditions, ceremonies, and knowledges that are handed down and present which we cannot touch. The convention is often compared to the Intangible Heritage designated in Korea but has a wider scope encompassing all areas of culture.

Memory of the World program is aimed at enlisting important documentary heritage of the world. Text, scores, archives, images, acoustic data, and even digital archives are within the range of the program.

All heritage recognized by the three programs are oftentimes referred as UNESCO World Heritage. However the name "World Heritage" is a proper name which refers only to the heritage enlisted upon the basis of the World Heritage Convention.

volcano, the abundant and diverse carbonate speleothems inside the impressive series of lava tubes, and the features of Seongsan Ilchulbong exposing all the important elements of a tuff cone.

Although there are a number of natural phenomenons and variety of flora and fauna present in Jeju, the botanical and ecological values were not included in the World Heritage justification. The geological features and elements caused by a volcanic eruption were thought to have an important global value. Therefore planting grass or trees on the surface of Seongsan Ilchulbong for a scenic presentation of the heritage would be a project completely disregarding the Outstanding Universal Value recognizing the geological features.

In order to protect the five lava tubes consisting a large part of the property, the government is continuously purchasing the land above the lava tubes, even though the caves are underground. Why is the land above the caves so important? As the justification spells out, the abundance and diversity of the secondary carbonate speleothems inside the lava tubes are very valuable. The gorgeous stalactites and stalagmites were formed when the sand from above slowly dissolved into the ground with rain water. If the land above the tubes were owned by an individual who might construct a building or start to cultivate the land and apply fertilizers, the caves would be exposed to a completely different environment and change. This shows how importatnt it is to know what to protect and how to protect it.

Is the heritage real? Are all parts of the heritage intact?

In the case of natural heritage it is relatively difficult to maneuver or change the values of heritage as humans wish to. However in the case of cultural heritage, it is slightly different. Determining the authenticity of the heritage comes in at this point. Sungnyemun Gate of Seoul City provides a good example. After the gate was burnt down and reconstructed, many professed the view that the gate had lost its authenticity as a cultural heritage. It was based on the doubt that the gate was now a structure not upholding the original values as it was built with new materials and in many parts with new technological methods. Indeed this is the process of determining the authenticity of a heritage. However material is not the only factor of determining authenticity. Many other factors such as form and design, materials and substance, use and function, traditions, techniques, and management systems, location and settings, languages, other forms of intangible heritage, spirit and feeling, and other internal and external factors need to be considered when determining the authenticity of a heritage.

On the other hand there is the condition of integrity. A heritage may have outstanding universal value but if an important part has been lost or is irreplaceable it is difficult to say that the heritage is intact or is presented as a whole. A good example is the Haeinsa Temple Janggyeong Panjeon, Depositories for the *Tripitaka Koreana* Woodblocks. As World Heritage is only applicable to immovable heritage it is the depository buildings holding the woodblocks and not the actual *Tripitaka Koreana* Woodblocks that are inscribed.

One of the frequent questions that pop up in school exams ask whether it is the woodblocks or the depositories that are inscribed on the World Heritage List. The question is intended to test whether or not the students know that the World Heritage Convention only applies to immovable heritage. However considering the integrity of the heritage, without the woodblocks the Janggyeong Panjeon would be rid of its purpose, function and point of existence. Therefore it is a better approach to consider the depositories holding the woodblocks as being inscribed on the World Heritage List.

Tourism, adaptive reuse, protection : Three interlocking wheels

As World Heritage gained popularity and the heritage inscribed on the list became famous, unexpected side effects began to arise. World Heritage properties started to be considered as certified heritage where all visitors and tourists must visit when travelling to a certain country. Heavy concentration of visitors make it difficult to maintain the protection of the heritage. Nonetheless for the sound protection and good adaptive reuse of the heritage, heritage tourism is a factor that is most needed as long as it is controlled. Tourism benefits the heritage economically by having the visitors bear a certain portion of the budget needed for the conservation, and at the same time provides the heritage with a social function. The more the local residents benefit from economic profits earned through the heritage, the higher the status of the heritage will become within the community. This can lead to a positive link of ensuring sound protection of the heritage. The ultimate purpose of protecting heritage is to hand it down to the next generation and share the values. Tourism is a very effective way of sharing the heritage values with a greater number of people.

This is why it is compulsory to establish rigid tourism plans when the heritage strives to get enlisted or at least immediately after it becomes World Heritage. Tourism must be controlled so that it can function as a method not to promote the heritage to a wider public and also to ensure actual protection of the heritage. Controlling visitors does not merely mean regulating number of visitors or method of entrance. Plans must be made on what information the visitors receive and what experiences they go through when they visit the heritage. Messages conveyed through the heritage must also be designed carefully.

Use of the heritage also needs to be thought out well. A structure or a place needs to have an independent function separate from being protected as a heritage. A space or a building without a proper function rapidly deteriorates. A house is maintained the best when somebody lives in it and quickly becomes dilapidated when it is empty. Like this, adaptive reuse of the heritage is not a grand or complicated task. It is to give an appropriate function to the heritage fitting within the society. A building can perform many different functions as a house, office, a place for gathering, or maybe an exhibition hall. Such roles of the heritage must be included in the overall conservation and management plan. The functions must also be options which best reflect the values of the heritage.

Looking through the lens of World Heritage : Cherishing the shared memory and heritage around us

Values of heritage are inherent in all heritage around us, in all remains of culture. It must not be thought that World Heritage properties are the only heritage that possess such unique and great values that cannot be found in other heritage. A property showing the epitome of a certain culture is formed on the basis of the countless layers and elements preceding it, and must be interpreted within such flow of culture.

All memories comprising the history of a culture must be considered equally important. A property possessing the precious memory of a village becomes the heritage of the village, and a property embodying the shared memory of a nation becomes the heritage of the country. In order for the national heritage to be formed, the experience and memory of each village and town must be valued. In other words, World Heritage is a way of protecting the memory and wisdom shared by all. Learning about different heritage enables people to understand and accept differences and diversity. Learning about the size, form and style of different properties are important too but efforts to read the thoughts and experience of the history and people when visiting a heritage can also greatly heighten the values of the property.

More Information

Convention Concerning the Protection of the World Cultural and Natural Heritage, UNESCO, 1972, http://whc.unesco.org/en/conventiontext

Operational Guidelines for the Implementation of the World Heritage Convention,

UNESCO, 2012, http://whc.unesco.org/en/guidelines

Advisory Body Evaluation for the Jeju Volcanic Island and Lava Tubes, IUCN, 2007, http://whc.unesco.org/archive/advisory_body_evaluation/1264.pdf

Advisory Body Evaluation for the Royal Tombs of the Joseon Dynasty, ICOMOS, 2009, http://whc.unesco.org/archive/advisory_body_evaluation/1319bis.pdf

World Heritage Centre, World Heritage: Challenges for the Millenium, UNESCO, 2007

The countless dolmens in this land

Gochang, Hwasun and Ganghwa Dolmens

Sim Joon Yong (A&A Research Institute of Culture)

World Heritage Dolmens

The Korean Peninsula is renowned for its high concentration of dolmens all over the world. The dolmens of Gochang in Jeollabuk-do Province, Hwasun in Jeollanam-do Province and Ganghwa in Incheon City, were inscribed on the World Heritage List in 2000 amongst the abundant megaliths occupying the country. The heritage fulfills criterion 3 for bearing a unique or at least exceptional testimony to a cultural tradition or to a civilization which is living or which has disappeared.

Hundreds of dolmens form clusters in the three areas, and the form and style are diverse, which make the dolmens important heritage in understanding the thoughts and techniques of the people who made them.

Dolmen

Dolmens are megalithic tombs or altars made in the prehistoric eras. They were often used as tombstones or monuments indicating a mass grave. In the Korean Peninsula and the neighboring areas, dolmens were generally constructed during the Bronze Age when the Kingdom of Gojoseon was in power (from 2,000 BCE to 300 BCE). Dolmens and mandolin-shaped bronze daggers are concentrated in areas conjectured to have been ruled by Gosjoseon, indicating the domains of the ancient kingdom.

Table style dolmen

Support style dolmen

Cover stone style dolmen

Surrounding stone style dolmen

Table style dolmen

Dolmens are commonly found in Europe, India and Southeast Asia, whilst it is rather scarce in China and Japan. The construction period and style are different from region to region, but generally 2, 4, or 10 flat stones are erected to support a larger stone cover on top.

Why is the Korean Peninsula filled with dolmens?

Approximately 40,000 dolmens are dispersed in Northeast Asia, accounting for almost half of the world's existing dolmens. Recent surveys have confirmed that there are dolmens found in India as well. The reason for such concentration has been the question for many scholars, but it still remains unanswered.

Gochang Dolmens, the densest dolmen cluster in the world

Dolmens erected around 4~5th centuries BCE are clustered in high concentration in Gochang. In an area spanning approximately 1,800m east to west, there are 447 dolmens clustered together. From smaller ones weighing less than 10 tons to the much larger ones weighing 300 tons, the whole variety of table types, go-board types, above ground stone coffin types can be seen. A park and museum has been created in the area making the visit to the dolmens more convenient and fun, with a small train to ride around the park with ease.

Hwasun Dolmens, dolmens to touch

Approximately 500 dolmens are scattered along a 10km valley. Quarries are also found nearby telling us the techniques

Dolmens of Gochang

Gochang Dolmen Museum

Inside of the Gochang Dolmen Museum

Pit dwelling replica in Gochang

used in processing the stone, constructing the dolmens and moving the large heavy stones. An exhibition center at the entrance also provides information with an in-situ excavation site of a dolmen.

Ganghwa Dolmens, looking more reliable than ever

Around 150 dolmens are located in the mountain ranges of Ganghwado Island. The largest dolmen in Korea, the Bugeun-ri Dolmen is located here. Formed in the table style, it measures 6.4m in length and 2.5m in height. There are about 10 clusters in

Dolmen Exhibition Center in Hwasun

Dolmen of Hwasun

Inside of the Exhibition Center

Stone quarry of Hwasun dolmens

Ganghwa and each cluster has different sizes and styles making the tour more interesting. A museum and a park is established alongside Bugeun-ri Dolmen. Ganghwado Island is filled with numerous historic heritage sites other than the dolmens adding to the enjoyment.

Hands-on experience corner in Hwasun

Osang-ri Dolmen in Ganghwa

Bugeun-ri Dolmen of Ganghwa

Jeomgol Dolmen in Bugeun-ri, Ganghwa

The four representative types of dolmens

Table style dolmen : This type has a stone chamber made with 3 or 4 flat slabs of stone standing on the ground with a large and wide stone covering the top, resembling the shape of a table. Extra large sized table style dolmens are found in the Liaodung Peninsula or along the riverside of Daedonggang River in Korea. They are usually located in hills or on mid-levels of mountains standing alone. Northern dolmens are rather small with a narrow stone chamber and a thick covering stone.

Support style dolmen : This type has a stone chamber made underground with flat or small stones surrounded with 4 to 8 supporting stones and a boulder covering the top. Usuallly the top boulders are immensely large and sometimes the dolmens lack chambers.

Cover stone style dolmen : Dolmens with the burial chamber made underground directly covered with a capstone are widely distributed in the Liaodung Peninsula, Korea and the Kyushu region of Japan.

Surrounding stone style dolmen : This type of dolmen has several natural or slab type rocks surrounding the capstone. The natural rocks encircle the capstone of a small dolmen as if forming a square or circular burial chamber. Those made with stone slabs have 6 to 12 slabs surrounding the edges of the capstone with one side left open.

Tips for enjoying the dolmens

1. Try to classify the dolmens into types. Is it a table type or a support type?
2. Ancient people used to draw pictures on dolmens or make grooves and, holes called Seonghyeol on the dolmens. Look closely for these details.

3. Most of the dolmens are accompanied by information boards. The information tells us about the artifacts excavated from the dolmen.
4. Where did the people obtain the material to build dolmens? Visit the quarries nearby.

What can you find inside a dolmen?

Some dolmens reveal many artifacts when they were excavated, but some have none. Items such as stone daggers, stone knives, stone arrow tips, red grinded pottery, eggplant pattern pottery, bronzeware, jade, stone chisel, whetstone, bedstones for grinding, spindle disc and fishnet weights have been excavated from dolmens.

The strength of 200 people is needed to erect a dolmen

Experimental archaeology has determined the number of people needed for moving the capstone. 16 to 20 people are needed to move a 1 ton stone over a mile (1.6km). Likewise 200 people are needed to move a 32 ton stone using round logs and ropes. In order to move the capstone, round logs have to be placed on the ground alternately in two rows. Ropes are tied on the to capstone, and it is moved b pulling the ropes or using levers. Levers and shoulder carrying would have been used for carrying relatively light stones on short distances, whereas the pulling method would have been employed for the heavier stones and longer distance moves. Once the capstone arrived at the tomb location, the burial chamber or supporting stones would have been covered with earth and soil to form a ramp. The capstone would be placed on top of the supports over the earthen ramp which would be removed once the stone was placed properly. The traces of earth filling the space in between the capstone and supporting stones are evidence of the usage of this method.

Stone quarries are found in the areas of Hwasun and Gochang. They are usually located at a higher spot than where the dolmens are erected. Naturally it would have been much easier to roll down a large boulder rock from the top than to pull it up from below.

More Information

A guide to historic explorations – Gyeongju, Korean Cultural Heritage Exploration Association, Dolbegae, 2008

UNESCO World Heritage in Korea, Jeju National Museum, Seogyeong, 2007

World Cultural Heritage of Korea I, Song Myeongseok, Park Jaeho, Kim Eunju, Banseok Publishers, 2013

UNESCO World Heritage, Korean National Commission for UNESCO Website http://www.unesco.or.kr/heritage

Encyclopedia of Korean Culture, http://terms.naver.com/list.nhn?cid=392&categoryId=392&categoryType=dictionary

A glimpse into the world view of Goguryeo

Complex of Goguryeo Tombs

Lee Jun Sung (Yonsei University)

(* Goguryeo and Koguryo both refer to the same kingdom of 高句麗, only romanized differently in South and North Korea.)

How many World Heritage are there in North Korea (official name the Democratic People's Republic of Korea)? Currently there are two, the Complex of Koguryo Tombs and Kaesong Historic Areas. Compared to South Korea (official name the Republic of Korea), the total number is very small and there are many complicated reasons why the heritage in North Korea are not well represented to the world.

The Complex of Koguryo Tombs in North Korea was inscribed on the World Heritage List on 1st July 2004, during the 28th session of the World Heritage Committee. It was the first heritage of North Korea to be inscribed on the list, eversince North Korea ratified the Convention in July 1998. The submission of the heritage on the Tentative List, together with six other properties were made in May 2000.

The capital city of the powerful East Asian kingdom of Goguryeo was based in Guonei City along the Apnokgang River (Yalu River) for 400 years, but King Jangsu relocated the capital

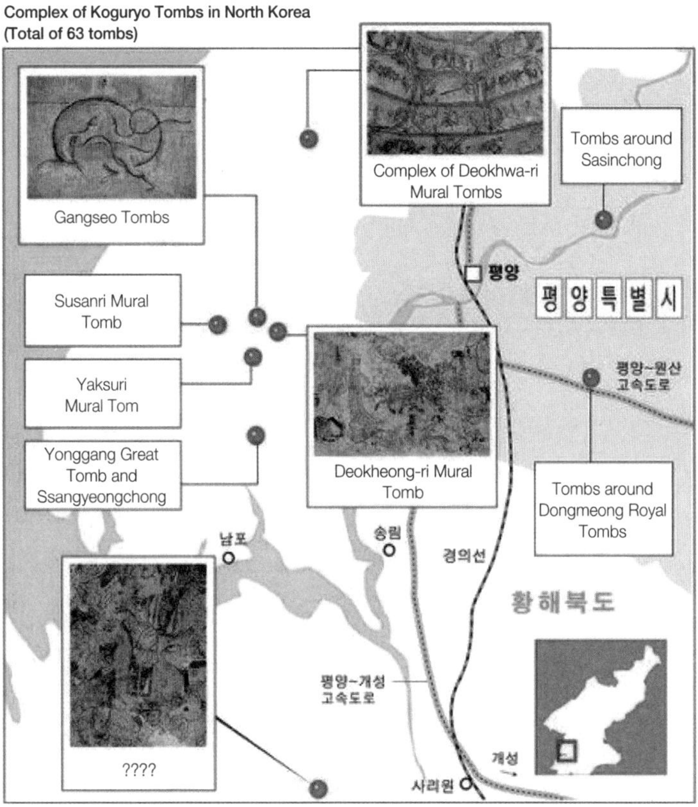

Map of Complex of Koguryo Tombs

city to Pyongyang in 427. This is the reason why Goguryeo tombs are concentrated in areas of Pyongyang and its vicinity in Nampo City, Pyeongannam-do Province and Hwanghaenam-do Province. A total of 63 tombs including the tomb of King Dongmyeong compose the heritage. 16 out of the 63 are mural tombs.

The tombs of Goguryeo in and around Pyongyang started to be investigated from the 1910s by Japanese scholars. Gangseo Great Tomb, Gangseo Mid Tomb, Yonggang Great Tomb and Ssangyeongchong in Nampo City started to be investigated in 1911, and in 1916 research started on the Four Deities Tomb in Honam-ri of Pyongyang. Slightly later in 1949 after the Korean liberation, Anak Tombs No. 1, 2 and 3 in Hwanghaenam-do Province were investigated and attracted a high level of attention. Deokhwa-ri Tomb No. 1, 2 and 3 in Daedong-gun County, Pyeongannam-do Province were properly excavated in 1976. As such, Goguryeo tombs in the Pyongyang area were continuously studied and investigated for a period of 100 years. New tombs dating from the Goguryeo period are still being found and investigated in this area.

UNESCO evaluated the murals of Goguryeo to "constitute masterpieces of the art of wall painting, with the subject matter offering unique evidence of the richness and complexity of the now-vanished Goguryeo culture." Also in terms of architectural

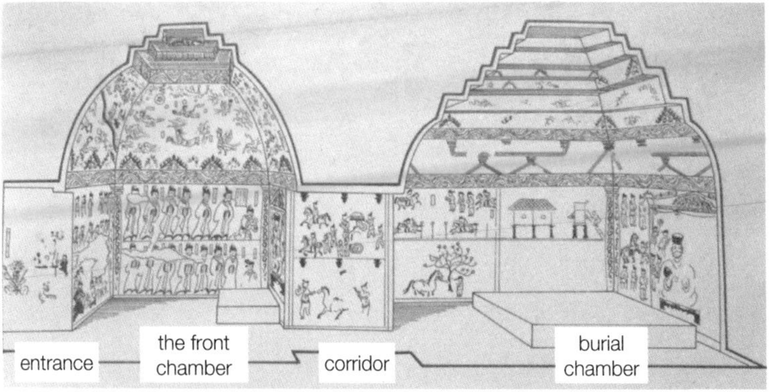

Three-dimensional drawing of Deokheung-ri Mural Tombs from the west
ⓒ Northeast Asian History Foundation

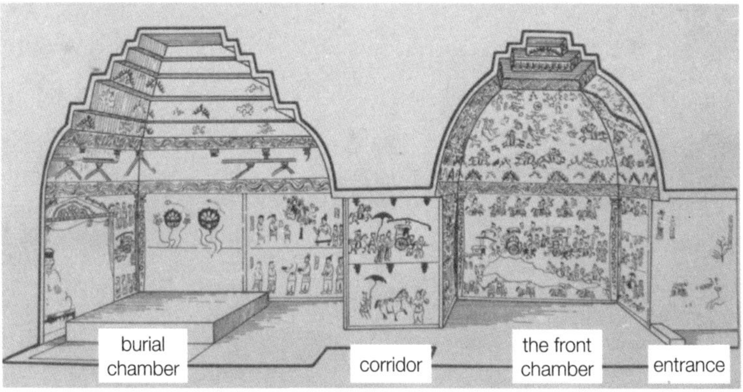

Three-dimensional drawing of Deokheong-ri Mural Tombs from the east
ⓒ Northeast Asian History Foundation

engineering it was valued that the tombs show "effective division of space and the technology employed represented a unique, creative and long-sought engineering solution to the technical problems posed by underground tomb construction." The tombs were noted for their "important influence on the burial customs of neighboring countries including those of Japan while representing an exceptional testimony to the Goguryeo culture, its burial customs, daily life and beliefs."

Features of Goguryeo Tombs

Goguryeo had many unique types of burial. The tombs can be largely classified into two types of the 'stone mound tomb' and the 'stone chamber tomb with a corridor'. Stone mound tombs were constructed with the body placed on the ground or in a pit, being covered with rubbles of stone to create the mound. On the other hand stone chamber tombs with a corridor were constructed upon the belief that tombs represent the living space of the dead. They were equipped with a corridor and an entrance so that people could enter and exit on foot. Stone mound tombs show the culture of lowering the body vertically from top to bottom in the burial, while the stone chamber tombs show a development in burial culture which led to the change in tomb structure with the body entering the tomb horizontally through a corridor.

Scholars believe that royals and nobility of Goguryeo were buried in stone mound tombs during the early years of its history but with the passing of time, stone chamber tombs with earthen mounds, and murals painted inside the chambers became more popular. This is supported by the fact that stone mound tombs are more commonly found in the Guonei City area on the northern side of the Apnokgang River in the earlier capital, whereas in the second capital of Pyongyang, stone chamber tombs are much more common. As the structure of stone chamber tombs allow space for wall paintings, many Goguryeo tombs from the Pyongyang area reveal fascinating and artistically unique murals.

Why are the Goguryeo tombs important?

Through the legacy of the Goguryeo people, especially the mural tombs, we can picture the life of the Goguryeo people. Goguryeo people had the pride of being the descendants of heaven, and integrated various neighboring cultures and ethnic

Stone mound ceiling of Deokhwa-ri Tomb No.2
© Northeast Asian History Foundation

groups to create a worldview which centered on Goguryeo. The astronomical chart on the ceiling of Jinpa-ri Tomb No. 4 in Pyongyang and Deokhwa-ri Tomb No. 2 in Daedong, Pyeongannam-do Province provide an intellectual conjecture on the level of astronomy. These are important materials which must be studied in depth in comparison with the Reproduced Stone Celestial Chart manufactured in 1395 during the early years of Joseon.

People of Goguryeo wished to carry on their daily lifestyle even after death. The tomb murals found within North Korea show the lifestyle of the Goguryeo people who reached the peak of their culture after they relocated the capital to Pyongyang. The clothes and attire of the nobility and commoners, music

Three-dimensional drawing of Anak Tomb No.3
ⓒ Northeast Asian History Foundation

A portrait in Anak Tomb No.3 ⓒ Catalogue of Joseon ruins and relics

and dance, religion, astronomy, daily tools and customs which cannot be confirmed through written records are all condensed and found in the tomb murals.

Deokheung-ri Tomb in Nampo City was built in resemblance to an actual house with the parlor for official meetings of the tomb occupant, inner chambers for the household, living room and bedroom with drapes. The image of the tomb occupant depicted in a daily living scene is shown in great detail. Also beside each scene on the walls and ceiling, names of official posts or explanations are written in ink providing evidence as to the birthplace and conduct of the tomb occupant. Extensive debate is still ongoing regarding the existence and reality of

Gangseo Great Tomb, White Tiger
ⓒ Northeast Asian History Foundation

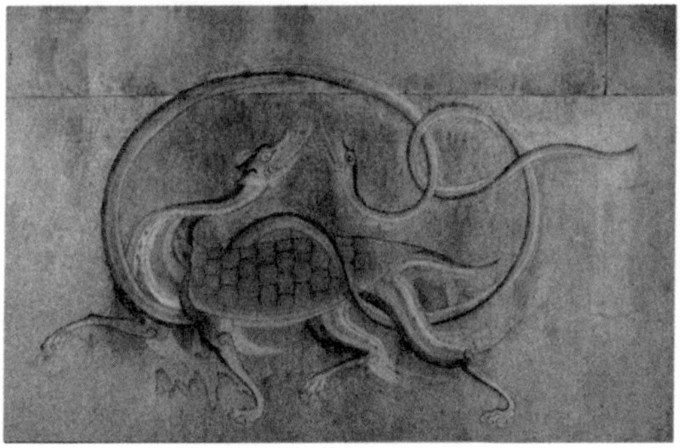

Gangseo Great Tomb, Black Tortoise
ⓒ Northeast Asian History Foundation

the Yuju Jasa, the name of one of the tomb occupant's actual official post.

The kitchen structure of a high ranking Goguryeo aristocrat can be seen in Anak Tomb No. 3. The kitchen is equipped with a steamer placed on a furnace that is connected to the fireplace and chimney; the butchery has meats of deer, pheasant and pork hanging about; the barn is occupied by a cow with a nose

Gangseo Great Tomb, Blue Dragon
© Northeast Asian History Foundation

Gangseo Great Tomb, Red Phoenix
© Northeast Asian History Foundation

ring; and there are depictions of a well. Scenes such as the tomb occupant being served by his servants whilst sitting together with his wife, hunting scenes with people riding horses, soldiers marching to the beat of the military band all reveal the strong and aspiring spirit of the Goguryeo people.

The Four Deities mural of Gangseo Great Tomb in Nampo City offer a view on the high artistic culture of Goguryeo. The artistic depiction of the Four Deities composed of the Blue Dragon, White Tiger, Red Phoenix and Black Tortoise are very much similar to the arts of China. Despite such similarities, the murals are considered one of the greatest paintings of East Asia from the 6-7th century with refined elegance and grace. These murals also influenced the paintings in Takamatsu Tomb

Gangseo Great Tomb

ⓒ Catalogue of Joseon ruins and relics No. 6

of Japan, demonstrating that the murals of Goguryeo played a pivotal role in the development of mural culture in East Asia.

Past and Present of Gogyuryeo Tombs in North Korea

The Capital Cities and Tombs of the Ancient Koguryo Kingdom in China was inscribed on the World Heritage List in 2004, at the same time when the Complex of Koguryo Tombs in North Korea was inscribed. North Korea had exerted efforts for a long time to inscribe the Koguryo tombs as World Heritage but was competitively challenged by China opposing the exclusive inscription of the site. In the end both States Parties agreed to inscribe the Koguryo heritage within their territory separately which resulted in the two different sites of Koguryo history being inscribed individually.

The Goguryeo site in China is composed of much more diverse and numerous types of heritage covering a wider area. Wunu Mountain City, Guonei City and Wandu Mountain City are the three cities included together with 40 tombs (14 royal tombs and 26 noble tombs). The simultaneous inscription of the Goguryeo sites is of course a positive confirmation of the outstanding values of the culture of Goguryeo. However for the inscription, the government of China refurbished the first and second capital city sites in Huanren and Jian at the national level. This was in line with the historic distortion attempt to

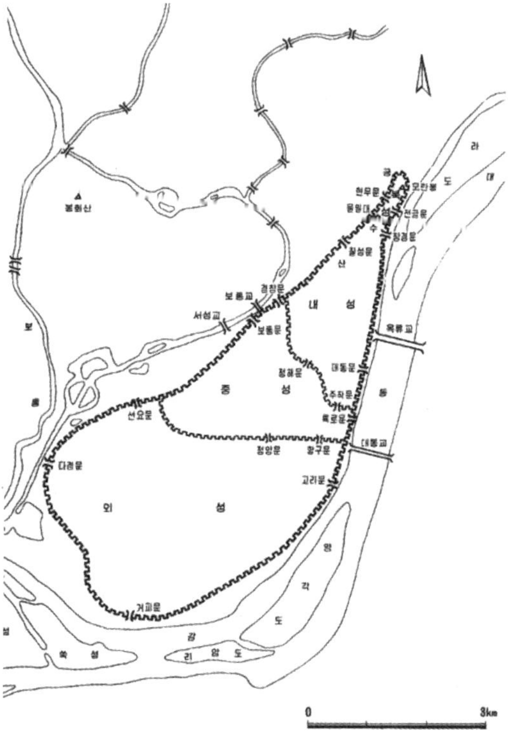

Pyongyang City Walls © Northeast Asian History Foundation

incorporate the history of Goguryeo into the history of China.

There are many diverse heritage sites which demonstrate the prime time of Goguryeo in Pyongyang besides the mural tombs. Pyongyangseong Fortress is an outstanding heritage displaying grandness and high quality engineering. Other sites near Pyongyangseong Fortress such as Daeseongsanseong Mountain Fortress, Cheongamri Earthen Fortress, Anhakgung,

Jeongneungsa and Gwangbeopsa Temples are only a few examples. These heritage must be protected and conserved respecting international standards so that efforts to additionally inscribe them can be continued.

Goguryeo historic sites including tombs and fortifications are continuously being discovered near Hantangang, Imjingang and Hangang Rivers in Korea. Therefore the study of Goguryeo sites must be carried out in consideration of the mid regions of the Korean Peninsula together with the sites found in the northern parts of Korea and the three northeast provinces of China.

More Information

Study on Goguryeo Mural Tombs, Jeon Hotae, Sagyejeol, 2000

A study on Goguryeo Tombs, Kang Hyeonsuk, Doctoral dissertation, Seoul National University, 2000

Conservation and management of Goguryeo mural tombs in North Korea, Journal of Korean Ancient History Vol. 25, Korean Ancient History Research Association, 2002

World Heritage Goguryeo Tombs, Baeksan Journal Vol. 70, Baeksan Society, 2004.

Conciseness and simplicity, ultimate beauty

Baekje Historic Areas

Baek Gil Nam (Seoul Baekje Museum)

Baekje Kingdom, Become a world heritage

Baekje Historic Areas is a heritage from the Baekje Kingdom, spread out in Gongju, Buyeo, and Iksan. It consists of 8 sites, which are Gongsanseong Fortress and Songsan-ri tombs from Gongju, Busosanseong Fortress and Gwanbuk-ri Archaeolgical Site, Jeongnimsa Temple Site, Naseong Outer walls, Neungsan-ri Royal Tombs in Buyeo, and Wanggung-ri Site and Mireuksa Temple Site in Iksan.

Baekje Historic Areas fulfilled criteria (ii) and (iii) to be inscribed on the World Heritage List. The values of Baekje building techniques and expansion of Buddhism through active interchange between Korean, Chinese, and Japanese ancient kingdoms were recognized. Also the capital city locations, Buddhist temples, fortress and buildings, tombs and stone

Busosanseong Fortress © Buyeo National Research Institute of Cultural Heritage

pagodas of Baekje Historic Areas show the history, afterlife views and religions, building techniques, artistic beauty being exceptional evidence of Baekje's history and culture.

The interaction that Baekje had with surrounding countries, shown through the building techniques of fortresses, palaces, temples and originality of religious culture have been highly merited.

The eight sites are all main factors consisting a capital city. The capital city system of East Asia had originated from China, which spread to surrounding countries and developed in their own styles. The capital city consists of the palace for the royal family; outer fortress walls called Naseong, which provided delineation for the residents; religious institutions which supported the ruling ideology; and royal tombs, symbolizing the royal authority. The individual eight sites correspond to these factors consisting the capital cities of Baekje.

What are the qualities of Baekje heritage? According to 『*Samguk sagi* (Chronicles of the Three Kingdoms)』 the palaces of Baekje were frugal yet austere, glamorous but not extravagant. In written records, elements of Baekje were all simple and concise. This refinement became its own beauty, which cannot be described in words. The ultimate beauty without excess is its attraction.

The Age of Rehabilitation_Gongju (Ungjin)

30,000 soldiers from Goguryeo captured Hanseong in AD 475, which was the capital city of Baekje. King Gaero of Baekje was caught and killed. His younger brother, who succeeded him became King Munju and transferred the capital to Ungjin, which is now known as Gongju. The choice of location is found from its geographical features. The north is protected by Chapyung Mountains, east by Gyeryongsan Mountain, and Geumgang River flows around the center of Gongju. It was a optimal defense area in case of another attack of Goguryeo.

In addition to its geographical feature, the major powerful clans based in Gongju had close political relationships with the central government of Baekje. Exquisite gilt-bronze cap and gilt-bronze shoes, which were gifts bestowed to powerful clans from the king, were excavated from the ancient tomb located at Suchon-ri, Uidang-myeon, Gongju. These make it possible to conjecture that there could have been a powerful influence of these clans, which helped the rehabiliation of Baekje.

The royal family of Baekje settled at Ungjin, but faced many internal and external troubles. However they slowly recovered stability, and developed national power at the time of King

Gongju Suchon-ri Ancient Tomb gilt-bronze cap ⓒ Gongju National Museum

Gongju Suchon-ri Ancient Tomb gilt-bronze cap replica ⓒ Seoul Baekje Museum

Dongseong and King Muryeong, and restored the country's standing through international exchange with the Southern Dynasty of China. On the basis of these backgrounds, King Muryeong officially proclaimed the strength of Baekje. Ungjin Era continued for 63 years, and Baekje recovered from the capture of Hanseong and the murder of their king. It was a signal of Baekje's revival.

The remains of Baekje in Gongju are Gongsanseong Fortress, where the palace had been located, and Songsan-ri Royal Tombs, where tombs of the royal family remains. There are countless other Baekje remains scattered around the city of Gongju although they are not all included in the World Heritage property.

Gongsanseong Gongsanseong was a fortress of Baekje, and

was called Ungjinseong at the time of Baekje. It was a center of local government until the time of the Joseon Dynasty. The fall of Baekje, King Uija also stayed in the fortress for a short period. The rebellion of Kim Heonchang ended in Gongsanseong in AD 822, during the Unified Silla period, and King Injo evacuated to Gongsanseong when the rebellion of Yi Gwal occurred in 1624. It is a place of many historical events.

It is a fortress, which was built along the Geumgang River. It is located at an altitude of 110m, and Geumgang River flows immediately to the north. It was an earthen fortification at the time of Baekje, but some sections were replaced to stone during mid-Joseon. The fortress measures approximately 2.5m in height, 3m in width and 2,660m in length. The section with a dual structure of earthen fortification is about 735m long. There are four gates, Geumseoru at the west, Jinnamnu at the

Gongsanseong

south, Yeongdongnu at the east, and Gongbungnu at the north. The royal palace area, Imnyugak, and the pond, Manharu are located inside.

Since the 1980s excavation work has continued in search of Baekje's remains. A lacquered leather armor and horse armor were discovered at the water storage facility in 2011. The image of Gongsanseong in Baekje Age will be restored through continuous excavation work.

Songsan-ri Royal Tombs Songsan-ri Royal Tombs are tombs of the kings and the royal family. Seven tombs among approximately 10 tombs have been investigated. On the west side of the valley the tomb of King Muryeong and tombs No. 5 and 6 are places, whereas tombs No. 1 to 4 are located on the east side of the valley. Tombs No. 1 to 5 are all stone chamber tombs with a corridor on the east side of the tomb through which the body of the deceased was carried through. Tomb No. 6 and the

Memorial stone © Gongju National Museum

Tomb of King Muryeong are brick chamber tombs. Tomb No. 6 has a dual passage with arch ceilings, and a long rectangular-shaped chamber. There are seven lamp niches, and many murals inside the tomb.

The Tomb of King Muryeong was discovered by chance during construction works for the drainage of tombs No. 5 and 6 in July, 1971. It is constructed with lotus patterns bricks, and consists of a passageway and the chamber. The chamber is 4.2m long north to south, 2.72m long east to west, and 3.14m high. There are 28 types of bricks used in construction, and some of them are carved with words, such as Daebang(大方), Jungbang(中方), and Geubsa(急使). These are considered as a type of design code used to designate the place for each brick.

4,600 objects of 108 types were discovered from the tomb. Amongst them 17 were designated as National Treasure. The Tomb of King Muryeong is the only royal tomb from the Three Kingdoms Period which the buried person is known.

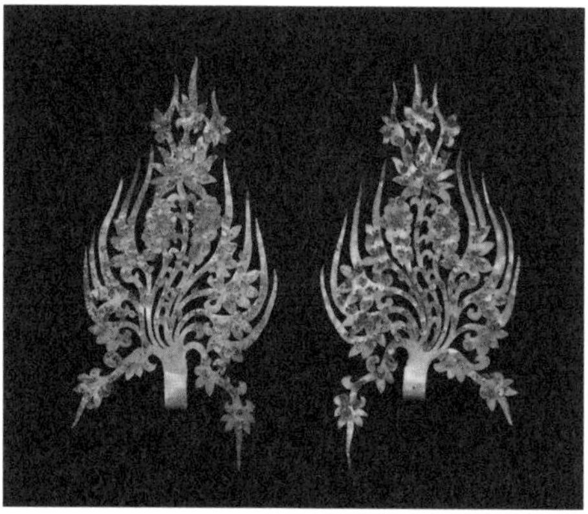

Gold diadem ornament © Gongju National Museum

Songsan-ri Ancient Tombs ⓒ Gongju National Museum

This is possible due to its memorial stone. The memorial stone is a precious remain which tells us the information about King Muryeong and the queen, and the production period of buried relics. A Chinese porcelain and the wooden coffin made by Japanese *Sciadopitys* show the relationship between Baekje and surrounding countries.

The moment of glory and despair_Buyeo (Sabi)

Buyeo, known as Sabi in the old days, is the third and last capital city of Baekje. King Seong of Baekje had transferred its capital from Ungjin to Sabi in AD 538. The transfer from Hanseong to Ungjin was due to the invasion of Goguryeo, but transfer from Ungjin to Sabi was Baekje's own choice.

One reason for transfer was the small and limited space of Ungjin as a capital. It was an advantageous location for defense, but it was too small for many people to live.

King Seong was strong and decisive and determined to relocate the capital. In all ages, transfer of capital city results in huge social conflict. Especially aristocrats having vested rights had to endure hardship of carrying all their life base. However King Seong had a dream of creating a new Baekje in his new capital that he designed. He even changed the name of the kingdom to Nam Buyeo.

There are many remains which reveal his strong will in Buyeo. He clearly

Five storied stone pagoda of Jeongnimsa Temple Site
ⓒ Buyeo National Museum

drew a distinct line between life and death with the construction of Naseong, and created a city space with clearly designed roads in direction of East-West and South-North. A capital city under a perfect order from the royal palace was created.

King Seong recovered Hangang River, which they had lost before, but he died in Gwansanseong Battle against Silla, and his dream of revival came to an end. His son, King Wideok carried on with the work. The capital city continued to expand and gave motivation for the development of a new capital, Iksan. However Sabi, which seemed to have a bright future, vanished in history in AD 660 simultaneously with the fall of Baekje.

Busosanseong Fortress and Gwanbuk-ri Site The Palace of Baekje is conjectured to have been in Gwanbuk-ri. Gwanbuk-ri is located at the north end of Buyeo city center, immediately outside Busosanseong Fortress. Buyeo has high ground to the north and is lower to the south. Therefore we can visually perceive all the city from Gwanbuk-ri. It is a great site for a palace. Busosanseong Fortress is located to the north, in Busosan Mountain. Busosanseong Fortress would have been the best location for emergency situations, such as threat of invasion. An extensive excavation in Gwanbuk-ri took place recently. Therefore roads, huge building sites, workshops, storage facilities, ponds from the period of Baekje were found, and this shows us the scope and scale of a Baekje palace.

Jeongnimsa Temple Site According to the Chinese history book 『Suseo』, many Buddhist temples and pagodas were erected in Sabi. To this day there are many temples sites, such as Jeongnimsa Temple Site, Gunsu-ri Temple Site, Seobuksa Temple Site of Busosan Mountain, Neungsan-ri Temple Site, and Wangheungsa Temple Site in Buyeo. The most representative one among them is Jeongnimsa Temple Site. Jeongnimsa Temple Site is located at the center of Buyeo city center, just south of the Gwanbuk-ri Site. There is a high possibility that the ancient road of Baekje from Gwanbuk-ri Site could be connected to the west wall of Jeongnimsa Temple Site.

The name, Jeongnimsa was derived from an excavated roof tile in 1942, with engravings indicating that the roof tiles were placed on the building in 1028, where the Tripitaka of Jeongnimsa were housed, during the reign of King Hyeonjong of Goryeo. During the excavation of 2008, it was confirmed that

Roof tile with engravings of Jeongnimsa © Buyeo National Museum

Jeongnimsa Temple Site © Buyeo National Research Institute of Cultural Heritage

the inner gate, pagoda, main building and assembly hall were located on a straight line on a north-south axis in Jeongnimsa Temple Site, and the site has a structure of one pagoda and one main building with a surrounding corridor. There is a pond located to the south of the pagoda.

The Five storied stone pagoda of Jeongnimsa Temple Site marks the epitome of pagoda building in Baekje. Until the 6th century pagodas were made of wood. Wooden pagodas could be built large and grand, but were very vulnerable to fire and disasters. Therefore people decided to build stone pagodas with high durability. The first example of it is the Mireuksa Temple site stone pagoda. It has the design of a wooden pagoda.

However the Five storied stone pagoda of Jeongnimsa Temple Site was built with a new form, escaping from the typical design of the past. This idea influenced the pagodas built afterwards, and the Five storied stone pagoda of Jeongnimsa Temple Site became a model for other pagoda structures.

A representative feature of Baekje, the Five storied stone pagoda of Jeongnimsa Temple site was sadly wounded with the fall of Baekje. Su Dingfang, the commander from Tang China engraved his military merits on the pagoda. The pagoda of Jeongnimsa Temple Site has shared all the glories and despairs of Baekje.

Naseong There is a Naseong outer city walls around Buyeo city. Naseong is a fortress surrounding the city. It was a defense facility and a delineation structure at the same time. It distinguished the inner and outer area of the capital, and also the space of life and death. The Neungsan-ri Royal Tombs was located to the east, on the outer area of Naseong.

Buyeo Naseong continues about 500m east to Cheongsanseong from Busosanseong Fortress, and curves south to Geumgang River.

The earthen fortifications of Naseong was constructed with Buyeop and Panchuk techniques. The exterior was constructed with stone. Buyeop technique is a construction method alternating between branches and soil to build a solid wall on soft ground to increase tensile strength. Panchuk technique hardens the ground by alternating soil and mud to build a solid wall. These techniques were conveyed to Japan from Baekje.

Neungsan-ri Royal Tombs Neungsan-ri Royal Tombs are located at the east side of Naseong. There are seven chamber tombs, and the representative one is tomb No. 2. Tomb No. 2 of Neungsan-ri has the same structure as the Royal Tomb of King Muryeong, but it is made of stone instead of bricks. This is the reason why it is considered to be the first tomb constructed in Neungsan-ri, and the buried person is assumed to be King Seong, who had transferred the capital to Sabi.

East walls of Naseong ⓒ Buyeo National Museum

Neungsan-ri Royal Tombs used elaborately processed stone, different from the ones used for the stone chamber tombs, which uses smaller rubbles of stones. This shows us the fact that the techniques for processing stones had improved. The construction style of Neungsan-ri Royal Tombs spread to local areas.

Neungsan-ri Temple Site is located between Buyeo Naseong and Neungsan-ri Royal Tombs. It consists of an inner gate, wooden pagoda, main building and assembly hall arranged on a straight axis from north to south, which is a typical one pagoda-one main building structure. Neungsan-ri Temple Site had been built by King Wideok to pray for the repose of King Seong, after his death in Gwansanseong battle. The Gilt-bronze Incense Burner and Stone Sarira Reliquary, which are considered to be the most representative heritage of Baekje, were discovered here. The stone sarira reliquary is an outer case for the sarira. It bears an inscription indicating that the princess, daughter of King Seong and younger sister of King Wideok had made the offering.

Gilt-bronze Incense Burner of Baekje has a cover, a body and a pedestal. The body is decorated with the lotus flower, and a dragon holds the body part at the pedestal. A phoenix is placed at the handle of the cover, and Bongraesan Mountain is depicted on the main body. There are a total of 12 holes, 10 holes on the cover, and 2 holes at the chest of phoenix for the smoke to come out. The vessel portrays an immortal world as the smoke comes out of the holes the incense is burnt. It is an exquisite heritage, demonstrating the spirit of Baekje.

A dream of restoration_Iksan (Geummajeo)

Iksan is a fertile land with vast fields, Geumgang River and Mangyeonggang River. It had been a local hub since the Bronze Age, and it was city of Geonmaguk, a small kingdom amongst Mahan. At Ipjeom-ri, Ungpo-myeon and Ungpo-ri to the west of Iksan, there is a Hanseong era tomb from the 5th century. Ipjeom-ri Tomb No. 1 is a stone chamber tomb, showing us the existence of powerful political influence through intricate and delicate burial goods such as the gilt-bronze cap and shoes, and Chinese celadon with four lugs.

Remains from the 7th century onwards, during the last days of of Baekje, are concentrated in Iksan. Iksan seems to have been developed as a capital or as a proposed site for capital during the reign of King Mu of Baekje. The relation between Iksan and King Mu appears to be very strong.

According to the history book, 『*Samguk Yusa* (Legends and History of the Three Kingdoms)』, a widow living by a pond located at the south of the capital had an affectionate relationship with a dragon and bore a son, whose name was Seodong.

Gilt-bronze Cap from Iksan Ipjeom-ri Acient Tombs ⓒ Jeonju National Museum

Five storied stone pagoda of Wanggung-ri

Seodong was a very devoted son, and he sold yams for living and took care of his single mother. Later he fell in love with Seonhwa, the princess of Silla, and became King Mu with her support. King Mu built Mireuksa Temple Site at Iksan.

As we can see, King Mu was born in Iksan, and when he became king, he dreamed of peace and prosperity in his kingdom with the foundation of a huge temple. His traces are still left at various places in Iksan. Maryongji is the birthplace of King Mu, Wanggung-ri, is conjectured to be the palace site, Mireuksa Temple Site was founded by King Mu and Princess Seonhwa, and the Twin Tombs are conjectured to be the burial places of the king and queen. Among them, Wanggung-ri Site and Mireuksa Temple Site are included in the Baekje Historic Areas.

Wanggung-ri Site Wanggung-ri Site is a palace of Baekje

Wanggung-ri Site © Buyeo National Research Institute of Cultural Heritage

which was constructed during the reign of King Mu. It is surrounded by walls stretching 492m south to north, and 234m east to west. There are 33 building sites in various sizes and layouts, including large buildings, garden facilities, support facilities, workshops and bathrooms.

Roof tile with engravings of Subu (capital city) © Buyeo National Museum

After the death of King Mu, temple buildings were constructed, and the five storied stone pagoda at the south of the site are evidence of these facts. The construction period of the five storied stone pagoda is debtaed and ranges from the period of Baekje to early Goryeo. Recently the opinion of the pagoda being constructed during Hubaekje is gaining strength, with the combination of the post-lintel single stylobate and flat roof style.

Glass Sarira bottle and gold box was discovered in 2009 from inside the five storied stone pagoda bearing similarities to the ones found from the west pagoda of Mireuksa Temple Site. It is therefore assumed to have been made during the reign of King Mu.

Approximately 4,000 objects of pottery, roof tile, glass, and gold articles were discovered from Wanggung-ri Site. There were also some roof tiles, engraved with words such as Gwangungsa(官宮寺), Daegwangungsa(大官宮寺), Wanggungsa(王宮寺). A roof tile engraved with the word Subu(首府, capital city) received attention. It indicates the living quarters of the king and central administrative organizations. It is a representative heritage which shows the power of Wanggung-ri Site.

Mireuksa Temple Site According to the history book, 『*Samguk Yusa* (Legends and History of the Three Kingdoms)』, Mireuksa Temple, located at the downside of Mireuksan Mountain, Iksan, was the largest temple site in East Asia. The inner gate, wooden pagoda, main building are located at the central section and a corridor surrounds it. There are also the east

and west sections, again containing inner gates, stone pagodas, main buildings, on both sides of the central section. To the north side of east and west section, the monastic quarters for the monks were connected to the main hall. A pond and waterway sits to to the south of the temple site. These correspond with the records from the book 『*Samguk Yusa*』. As remains dating from Unified Silla, Goryeo and Joseon are continuously found, we know that the history of Mireuksa Temple continued after Baekje.

The only remaining structure in Mireuksa Temple Site is the West Pagoda. There was a reinforcement work with cement during the Japanese colonial times. Serious safety problems arose

Sarira bottle from the West Pagoda of Mireuksa Temple Site
ⓒ National Research Institute of Cultural Heritage

and a large scale disassemblement and reassemblement work commenced in 1999. A stone sarira container was discovered under the central pillar stone, during the disassemblement of the pagoda in 2009. According to the golden sarira record which was found inside, the person who enshrined the sarira in the West Pagoda was the queen of King Mu, daughter of Jwapyeong(佐平) Sataekjeokdeok(沙宅積德). This evidence brought huge controversy. Before, it was widely known that Princess Seonhwa, daughter of King Jinpyeong had founded

Mireuksa Temple in accordance to the records in 『*Samguk Yusa*』. After years of debate, it is now widely believed that that King Mu had two queens. Princess Seonhwa was the source of Mireuksa Temple's foundation, and after its foundation, Queen Sataek built the west area including the West Pagoda.

Incompletion_Seoul (Hanseong)

Baekje had transferred its capital twice in order of Hanseong-Ungjin-Sabi. Then where is Hanseong, the first capital city of Baekje? According to the 『*Samguk Sagi* (Chronicles of the Three Kingdoms)』, the first capital started out from Wiryeseong, south of the Hangang River, and developed into Hanseong consisting of the North and South Fortresses. The royal tombs were known to have been constructed using the stones from Hangang River.

Wiryeseong, to the south of Hangang River, has similar geographical features to the earthen fortifications located at Pungnap-dong, Seoul. The location of the North and South fortresses corresponds to the earthen fortifications at Pungnap-dong and Mongchontoseong. There are currently five tombs preserved at Seokchon-dong, near Mongchontoseong Fortress, but according to the distribution map made by Japan in 1917, there were 293 stone mound tombs and earthen pit tombs around the areas of Seokchon-dong, Garak-dong, and Bangi-dong. The first capital of Baekje, consists of two royal fortresses and many

earthen fortifications in Pungnap-dong, Seoul © National Research Institute of Cultural Heritage

other tombs, can be found in Songpa-gu, Seoul. Baekje Historic Areas, which spans 500 years of history, does not include the heritage dating from the Hanseong Era. Although it is late, Seoul Metropolitan City is now making efforts to include the Baekje heritage of Hanseong to the World Heritage List. Hopefully in the near future, the heritage of the Hanseong Era will also be included as World Heritage.

More Information

Kim Ki-Seob, 「The Capital City and its Structure of Hanseong Age of Baekje」「The History and Culture of Hanseong, Baekje」, Seokyung Culture, 2007

Buyeo National Museum, Special Exhibition Workbook 「King Muwang of Baekje」, 2011

Baekje Historic Areas, World Heritage Nomination Office, 「Baekje Historic Areas Guidebook」, 2012

Gongju National Museum · Gongju City, 「An Explanation · Interpretation of Basic Data on Songsan-ri Ancient Tombs」, 2012

Gongju National University Museum · Gongju City, Gongju Historic City Preservation and Promotion Research Series 「Ungjinseong · Gongsanseong」, 2013

Jeonju National Museum, 2013, Special Exhibition Workbook 「Iksan」, 2013

Buyeo National Research Institute of Cultural Heritage, 2014, 「寺塔甚多, Buddhist Temples and Heritage from Sabi Era of Baekje」, 2014

Kwon Oh Young, 「The Value of Heritage from Hanseong, Baekje as World Cultural Heritage」「Emphasis of the Value of Heritage from Hanseong, Baekje as World Cultural Heritage」, Seoul Metropolitan City, 2015

Capital of Silla, ancient capital of the Unified Korean Peninsula

Gyeongju Historic Areas

Sim Joon Yong (A&A Research Institute of Culture)

Around 1st century BCE, the Korean Peninsula was divided into three kingdoms of Goguryeo, Baekje and Silla. Although Silla was the latest one to enter into advancement, it was the one to take initiative in unifying the three kingdoms in 676 CE. Gyeongju was the capital city of Silla from the very beginning and still embraces the entire history of the ancient kingdom of Silla which was the longest surviving kingdom in the Korean Peninsula spanning from BCE 57 ~ CE 935. After the demise of Silla, the capital of the peninsula moved to Gaeseong and Hanyang (current day Seoul), which paradoxically protected Gyeongju from greater development. The city was preserved with all its historic remnants as a time capsule, and welcomes visitors to all the various different heritage scattered in the city.

Gyeongju Historic Areas can be chronologically compared to the historic areas of Kyoto and Nara in Japan, and is highly esteemed for the density and variety of the types of heritage embedded in the areas. The heritage was inscribed on the World Heritage List by justifying criteria (ii) and (iii) for World Heritage inscription as having many sites and monuments of exceptional significance in the development of Buddhist and secular architecture in Korea. The heritage also bears outstanding testimony to the cultural achievements of Silla.

The entire property is divided into 5 areas. These are Mount Namsan Area, Wolseong Area, Tumuli Area, Hwangyongsa Temple Area and Fortress Area. There are more than 50 individual designated heritage within the World Heritage property.

Mount Namsan, the epitome of Silla Buddhist culture

Mount Namsan is known as the greatest outdoor museum of Korea, pristinely preserving the fascinating Buddhist culture of Silla. There are countless Buddhist and historic features in Namsan such as Najeong, the location of the founding myth of Silla; Poseokjeong where the last day of Silla was witnessed; the seated stone Buddha of Mireukgok Valley; Baeri standing stone Buddha statues; rock cut Buddha images of Chilburam and many more.

Najeong Well is known to be the birthplace of Bak Hyeokgeose, the founding father of Silla, and the well was recognized as an important site until the final days of the kingdom. An entry in the 『*Samguk Yusa* (Memorabilia of the Three Kingdoms)』 reads as follows.

> 2,000 years ago, there were six villages living in cooperation in the area of Gyeongju. The village head of Gohechon, witnessed a bright light shining upon the Najeong Well with a white horse next to it bowing towards the well. When he approached, a red egg could be seen in the place of the horse and from that egg the founding father of the kingdom, Bak Hyeokgeose was born.

Engravings of six Buddhas in Samneung Valley of Namsan

View of Gyeongju from Samneung Valley

Seated stone Buddhas of Samneung Valley

Buddhas of Samneung Valley

Najeong was initially considered as a mythical location rather than an actual place, but from excavation works that took place from 2002, many important sites were revealed. Three wells dating from the Silla Kingdom and an octagonal building site measuring 3,600㎡ in area with a well site underneath it have been confirmed, providing voluminous information about the beginning years of Silla.

Poseokjeong was a place of leisure and entertainment frequently visited by the king and his subjects. It is recorded in the 『*Samguk Yusa* (Memorabilia of the Three Kingdoms)』. In Poseokjeong, the game of floating a cup upon a curvy waterway was played. A cup filled with liquor would be placed in the waterway while everybody composed a poem using the suggested theme or character. Those that could not compose a verse of poem before the cup reached them had to drink up the liquor. The game is known to have originated from China but there are no sites of evidence found in China.

Poseokjeong is also the place where the end of the Silla Kingdom was witnessed. In the book 『*Dongguk Tonggam* (History of the Eastern Kingdom)』 there is an entry which describes the suicide of King Gyeongaewang (of Silla), who was captured by the men of Gyeonhwon from Hubaekje whilst he was drinking together with the court ladies in Poseokjeong.

There are almost 100 temple sites, 60 stone Buddha statues, 40 stupas formed within the 40 or so valleys of Mount Namsan. Most of these Buddhist art remaining in Namsan were produced during the Silla Kingdom demonstrating the devout Buddhist faith of the Silla people. These heritage also provide information for the restoration of other properties. In the rock-cut Buddha image cluster of Tapgok, there are engravings of a 9-story wooden pagoda and a 7-story wooden pagoda, both of which cannot be seen in actual form nowadays. These depictions are sources of valuable information in conjecturing the original shape of the 9-story wooden stupa of Hwangryongsa Temple.

Wolseong Area, the heart of the capital of Silla

Numerous sites are inside Wolseong area. Wolseong Fortress is where the royal palace of Silla was known to be located; Gyerim Forest is where Kim Alji, the founding father of the Silla royal Kim family was found inside a golden chest; Imhaejeonji Pond is where the luxuriousness of the Silla royal household can be seen; and Cheomseongdae which is conjectured to be the earliest astrnomical observatory in Asia are all clustered in

Stone Ice Storage of Wolseong

Imhaejeonji

Imhaejeonji at night

this area.

Imhaejeonji is also called Anapji. It is an artificial pond constructed immediately after the unification of the Three Kingdoms, and the compound consists of the pond and other palace facilities. Considered to be the epitome of Silla gardens, the pond has straight sides where palace facilities are located, but the sides which are viewed from the palace are formed in irregular lines providing various different views, making the pond appear much larger than its actual size. The scientific and high quality landscaping techniques of the Silla people can be fully appreciated from the compound.

Various artifacts were found from the pond during an excavation survey which included a 14-sided die called a Juryeonggu. The die was used in playing games during parties and penalties such as 'drink three glasses of liquor at once', 'sing a song as one wishes', and 'to dance without music' are written on the sides, giving us a glimpse into the entertainment culture of the days in Silla.

Daeneungwon, a royal tumuli park

Many tombs of the royal family of Silla such as the Hwangnam-ri Tomb Cluster, Nodong-ri Tomb Cluster and the Noseo-ri Tomb Cluster are located in Daeneungwon, the Tumuli Park. However tombs are not limited to the park area only. The large hill mounds of the tombs can be seen virtually all over Gyeongju. Many valuable artifacts attesting to the culture of Silla such as golden crowns, ornaments, painting of a heavenly horse on a saddle flap, glass cups, and various pottery were found from the tombs which have been excavated.

Amongst the tombs in Tumuli Park, Cheonmachong Tomb is the only one where a visitor can go inside. The tomb was lined with wooden panels to create a coffin which was then covered with piles of rubble and stone, The very top was covered with earth. Approximately 15,000 artifacts were excavated from Cheonmachong Tomb including a golden crown and a saddle flap. The saddle flap made of birch tree made to cover both

Daeneungwon Tumuli Cluster

Exhibition hall of the Cheonmachong inside Daeneungwon

Gwaereung, tomb of King Wonseong

Twelve zodiac statues surrounding Gwaereung

Stone statue of a military official with facial features of the people from Xiyu (Western regions beyond China)

sides of the horse's stomach has an image of a heavenly horse (*cheonma*, 天馬) which gave its name to the tomb.

Gwaereung, known to be the tomb of King Wonseong, has interesting stone figures guarding the king's tomb. The twelve zodiacs surrounding the tomb and the military official with distinct foreign features make the tomb more engaging and enjoyable to understand the burial style of Silla.

The grandest temple of all Silla, Hwangryongsa Temple

In Hwangryongsa Temple Area there were two temples, Hwangryongsa and Bunhwangsa. Hwangryongsa was known to be the grandest Buddhist temple of all Silla which was unfortunately burnt down during the Mongol invasions of the Goryeo Dynasty. Extensive excavation works have revealed the enormous and imposing scale of the temple. Artifacts numbering almost 40,000 are all invaluable material in studying the history of Silla.

East stupa of Mireuksa Temple site

The nine-story wooden stupa site attracts strong attention amongst the building sites within Hwangryongsa Temple site. The stupa was originally built in the hopes of defending the kingdom from the invasion of nine foreign countries. It was destroyed by the Mongol army that invaded Goryeo in 1283. The stupa was conjectured to have been 80m in height, and only the site where it stood remains.

Right next to Hwangryongsa Temple site is Bunhwangsa Temple. The brick style stone stupa is assumed to have been built in 634 together with the establishment of the temple. It is the oldest stone stupa dating from the period of Silla which is still kept intact.

The different customs of building stupas in China, Korea and Japan have roots from long held traditions. Brick stupas were popular in China, whereas Korean stupas were most commonly built with stone, while the Japanese preferred wood as the material for stupas. The regional features are caused from many

Bunhwangsa brick style stone stupa

Stone lion on Bunhwangsa brick style stone stupa

Seat of the giant gilt bronze Buddha statue in Hwangryongsa

Nine story wooden stupa site in Hwangryongsa

different given natural conditions. Certainly there are some examples of wooden stupas in China as there are brick stupas in Korea. The brick style stone stupa of Bunhwangsa becomes all the more interesting in this light. On closer look, the brick style stupa reveals its stone material which is processed to have a brick-like appearance. The excellent stone masons of Silla made the brick style stone stupa as they made an artificial cave grotto like Seokguram. A similar example can be found in the Mireuksa Temple site in Iksan in the neighboring kingdom of Baekje. The stone stupa found here bears the style of a wooden stupa. These examples of varying stupas distinctly show how different cultures and customs met each other and changed with the impact. The stone stupa of Bunhwangsa Temple was originally a much higher stupa with nine stories, but only three stories are kept intact.

Goguryeo and Baekje, the two other kingdoms which occupied the Korean peninsula together with Silla, also built grand fortresses encompassing their capital cities. However unlike the others, Silla only built mountain fortresses in military strongpoints. This appears to be relevant with the topography of Gyeongju which is surrounded by mountains. Of all the mountain fortresses that protected the capital of Silla, Myeonghwalsanseong Fortress is included in the World Heritage property.

Excavation site in Myeonghwalsanseong Fortress

Myeonghwalsanseong Fortress, defending the capital of Silla

The exact date of construction is unknown, but an entry in 『*Samguk Sagi* (Chronicles of the Three Kingdoms)』 remarks that Japanese soldiers attacked Myeonghwalseong in 405, which

Myeonghwalsanseong Mountain Fortress

indicates that the fortress was built before 405.

The fortress is about 6km in length. The walls consist of several different level of tiers. The lowest level has a slight angle and the outside wall is made of half processed stone. The very top is covered up with earth. The inside of the fortress walls are very strong being meticulously loaded with stone material.

At the time the fortress was constructed, Silla was frequently invaded by Goguryeo to the north and Japan to the southeast. Myeonghwalsanseong is conjectured to have been established to prepare for the intense and frequent Japanese invasions. The Japanese surrounded and attempted to conquer the fortress in 431, which shows that it was an important strategic point in defending Gyeongju.

Many parts of the fortress have collapsed and only partial areas reveal its old glories. These parts are possibly the reconstructed areas built during the reign of King Jinpyeongwang of Silla.

More Information

A guide to historic explorations – Gyeongju, Korean Cultural Heritage Exploration Association, Dolbegae, 2008

UNESCO World Heritage in Korea, Jeju National Museum, Seogyeong, 2007

World Cultural Heritage of Korea I, Song Myeongseok, Park Jaeho, Kim Eunju, Banseok Publishers, 2013

UNESCO World Heritage, Korean National Commission for UNESCO Website http://www.unesco.or.kr/heritage

Encyclopedia of Korean Culture, http://terms.naver.com/list.nhn?cid=392&categoryId=392&categoryType=dictionary

Creation of an ideal Buddhist Land in the capital of Silla

Seokguram and Bulguksa

Sim Joon Yong (A&A Research Institute of Culture)

Buddhism had utmost influence in Korea after it was introduced to the peninsula from India through China. Before the start of the Joseon Dynasty in 1392, Buddhism maintained its status as the state religion. Winning over battles against Goguryeo and Baekje and finally unifying the peninsula, Silla especially excelled in flowering classical and elegant Buddhist art. Silla imbibed diverse cultural elements that travelled across the Silk Roads, and created a unique Silla culture by reinterpreting the elements with grace and delicacy.

Seokguram Grotto is widely known for displaying the epitome of Silla culture. The overall heritage embodies every aspect of architecture, mathematics, engineering, geometry, religion and art, and even today it is not possible for us to emulate the same

Seokguram © Kim Taeshik

Seokguram in the early 20th century Catalogue of Joseon Antiquities and Sites

technical achievements of the construction.

Bulguksa Temple is a representative example portraying the Land of Buddha, an idealized world of the Buddhist religion. The entire complex of the exemplary Korean temple is incomparable to any other temple in its architectural uniqueness.

Both Seokguram Grotto and Bulguksa Temple were inscribed on the World Heritage List in 1995 as a masterpiece of East Asian art (criterion i) and as an outstanding example of Buddhist religious architecture as a material expression of the Buddhist belief (criterion iv).

A wish to have a stone cave in this land

Stone caves generally appear in extreme weather conditions, where it is very cold or very hot, and especially in dry regions. Cave temples with Buddhist statues inside can be most commonly found in the dry regions of India and China. Dunhuang Cave and Longmen Grottos are famous examples of cave architecture together with Petra in Jordan.

Caves were used as dwellings only until the Neolithic Age in the Korean Peninsula. There are many reasons why caves were not utilized so much, but it is mainly because the climate has distinct four seasons which creates a humid atmosphere inside the caves. It is also because most of the land is composed of

Model of Seokguram in the Silla History and Science Exhibition Hall

Protective shelter of Seokguram (photography is prohibited inside)

Seokguram seen from a distance

granite which is difficult to process and refine. Ever since the Bronze Age, caves were only utilized as storage or tombs where people did not have to spend long times.

Despite these conditions, the people of Silla constructed a temple in the form of a stone cave. Not in a natural cave but in a man-made construction. Why did they establish such a wonderful architectural masterpiece in a place so unsuited for the type?

To construct a dry grotto temple in Silla

The greatest concern to the people of Silla before they started the construction of Seokguram was most probably, 'how do we build a stone cave temple with a temperate atmosphere while controlling excess humidity?'

Seokguram displays the exact solution in every aspect of its construction. The grotto has been maintained for over a thousand

Bulguksa Temple

years since its construction in 774, proving that the people of Silla possessed knowledge and technique in producing constant thermal and humidity facilities utilizing the natural conditions.

Unfortunately however Seokguram was completely dismantled during the Japanese Colonial period, and has not been recovered in its original status even with today's advanced cutting edge science and technology. Isothermal and isohumidity machinery has been installed inside thick glass barriers separating the inside of the grotto from the natural outdoor environment and visitors. The modern day science and technology has clearly not been able to catch up to the level of the Silla minds from 1200 years ago. It is still a mystery how the people of Silla constructed Seokguram preserving the ideal climate conditions.

According to many experts, there is a high possibility that the trickling flow of water that encircled the grotto absorbed excess humidity, and the breeze that flowed through the vent on the walls played an important role in controlling the atmosphere. There is no flow of water and wind in the modern day Seokguram. Perhaps the experts of the future may be able to unravel the secret of control in Seokguram.

Composition of Seokguram

Seokguram is made of white washed granite on the mid level of Mount Tohamsan. Inside the man-made stone cave, Sakyamuni Buddha sits in the center surrounded with 39 sculptures of Bodhisattvas, disciples and heavenly deities. The cave has a rectangular antechamber and a circular main room connected by a corridor. In the rectangular antechamber the eight Dharmapalas are sculpted on both sides, four on each side. At the entrance two Vajrapanis adorn both sides of the wall and on the corridor the Four Heavenly Kings are sculpted on the walls, two on each side.

The entrance of the main chamber has eight cornered stone pillars on each side, and the Buddha sits in the center slightly towards the back. On the left and right sides of the entrance two devas, two Bodhisattvas and ten arhats fill the walls, and the eleven-faced Avalokitesvara stands immediately behind the main Buddha. All the sculptures inside Seokguram display the finest level of Silla masonry, rendering a phenomenal feeling to those that are viewing them.

Land of the Buddha, the delicate and beautiful Bulguksa Temple

Bulguksa Temple was built together with Seokguram and is on the east side of the road that leads to the sea from Gyeongju.

Seokgulam members

Together with Seokguram, the temple also shows wondrous and refined aesthetic qualities of Silla which reached its climax after unifying the three kingdoms.

Although now we can reach right up to the front gates of the temple by car, in the olden days one must have had to quietly walk through the forests of Mount Tohamsan, the highest peak in Gyeongju in order to get to the temple. The walk along the paths of the mountain would project calmness on those who headed for the temple and the image of the mystical religious architecture dawning upon the entrance as though it was floating on top of a grand pond would have deepened their piety and belief.

Bulguksa is composed of three distinct areas, the Daeungjeon Hall area (Hall of the Great Hero), Geuknakjeon Hall area (Hall of Paradise) and the Birojeon Hall area (Hall of Vairocana). Daeungjeon area is the center of the temple which can be reached by climbing up the staircase bridge of Cheongungyo (Bridge of Blue Clouds) and Baekungyo (Bridge of White Clouds) and entering through Jahamun Gate. The staircases were originally built over a large pond but the pond is no longer there, and visitors now have to enter through the side in order to protect the staircase bridges.

The main hall sits in front of Jahamun Gate and a lecture hall called Museoljeon is connected to it by corridors to the back. Two stupas standing in the courtyard of Daeungjeon Hall are the Seokgatap (Stupa of Sakyamuni) and Dabotap (Stupa of Many Treasures).

Seokgatap is recognized for the perfected gracefulness embedding the long tradition of Silla stone stupas. The exact and balanced proportion of the stupa starting from the supportive base to the top is often likened to a beautiful Silla woman.

While Seokgatap shows the zenith of Silla stupas, Dabotap displays a singularly exceptional form. Starting from the square shaped base varying into circular and octagonal forms to the top constitutes a totally different style from its neighbor.

As Daeungjeon is the hall for the Sakyamuni Buddha based on the Lotus Sutra, Geuknakjeon is the Paradise Land of the Amitabha Buddha of the Amitayurdhyana Sutra. Birojeon becomes the Buddha of the Lotus Land in suit of the Avatamsaka Sutra. The Buddhas of the past, present and future are therefore represented in each of the areas. The reason that Bulguksa encompassed all the popular Buddhist doctrines into its grounds was not only to complete the composition of the temple but to strengthen the solidarity of the state through the powers of the Buddhist religion. The motive must have been to comprehensively lay down each of the different sections and areas into a holistic complex in order to create a perfect Land of Buddha.

Natural and man-made beauty mixed in the stone terraces

Throughout its long history, Bulguksa struggled through numerous fires. Most of the wooden structure that currently stand on the grounds were reconstructed after the Joseon Dynasty. However the stone terraces and stylobates still preserve their original forms from the Silla Period.

The stone terraces are designed almost like wooden furniture where a frame is created with processed stone which is then filled with natural rocks and rubble that compose the entire terrace. The terraces alone tell us how much the people of Silla emphasized the importance of both natural and human elements.

The stone terraces were established in order to form a

Dabotap Stupa

Seokgatap Stupa

Stone terraces of Bulguksa dating from the Silla period

Who built Seokguram and Bulguksa?

Samguk Yusa has entries noting that Kim Daeseong constructed Seokguram Grotto and Bulguksa Temple. Kim Daeseong used to be a poor servant who lived with his widowed mother, but he worked hard to earn himself a living. One day he heard a Buddhist monk preach that those who made offerings to the Buddha will have a better next life, which prompted him to endow all his belongings to a temple.

Not long after, Kim Daeseong died, but that night in the household of Kim Munryang, a minister of Silla, a voice was heard saying that'Kim Daeseong of Moryang-ri will his wife gave birth to a son who was Kim Daeseong born once again. This time born as the son of an affluent household, Kim Daeseong grew up and constructed Seokguram Grotto for his mother of the previous life, and Bulguksa Temple for his parents of the present life.

This story tells us when the two temples were built. It also shows how the people of Silla thought about death and reincarnation. Seokguram Grotto and Bulguksa Temple started to be built in 751 and was completed in 774.

horizontal flat space for the buildings to be erected, as the temple sits on an angled slope of a mountain. Therefore looking at it from the side, the terraces become lower towards the back, but the frames are not completely horizontal and slightly tilted with a slope in order to create a natural diminution ratio.

More Information

A guide to historic explorations - Gyeongju, Korean Cultural Heritage Exploration Association, Dolbegae, 2008

UNESCO World Heritage in Korea, Jeju National Museum, Seogyeong, 2007

World Cultural Heritage of Korea I, Song Myeongseok, Park Jaeho, Kim Eunju, Banseok Publishers, 2013

UNESCO World Heritage, Korean National Commission for UNESCO Website http://www.unesco.or.kr/heritage

Encyclopedia of Korean Culture, http://terms.naver.com/list.nhn?cid=392&categoryId=392&categoryType=dictionary

Capital of Goryeo,

completing the unification of Korea

Kaesong Historic Areas

Nam Chang Geun (Gyeonggi Cultural Foundatuin)

By the end of the 10th century Silla was once again in turmoil and the land was again divided into the Later Three Kingdoms. Hugoguryeo, which succeeded Goguryeo, unified the Korean Peninsula in 918 and started the Goryeo Dynasty. Goryeo declared itself to be an imperial state like China and placed the capital in Kaesong. Goryeo ruled the Korean Peninsula for 475 years until 1392. The dynasty was very active internationally and formed close exchange relations not only with China, Japan but up to Arabia and Persia. The official English name of Korea has its roots from the name Goryeo, which became widely known to the Western world.

As the capital city, Kaesong was the political, social and cultural center over the entire history of Goryeo, holding

Kaesong City Map in the late Joseon(Kaesong Goryeo History Museum)

abundant cultural heritage. Kaesong provides valuable evidence as capital city of the medieval times being comparable to Chang'an in China, Nara in Japan and Citadel of the Ho Dynasty in Vietnam.

Kaesong Historic Areas is a property composed of various different heritage components demonstrating the ruling base of the Goryeo Dynasty (918-1392). The city design adapting to the natural terrain respecting pungsu geomancy principles, the royal palace and tombs signifying the authority of the state, the defensive fortress facilities, and Confucian cultural heritage

South Great Gate of Kaesong City

handed down from a period when the ruling ideology shifted from Buddhism to Confucianism are all properties embodying the cultural and spiritual values of the Goryeo times.

Kaesong was enlisted as World Heritage in 2013 fulfilling criterion (ii) and (iii). The evaluation of the site reads as follows. The heritage exhibits the assimilation of the cultural, spiritual and political values of the various states that existed on the Peninsula prior to Goryeo, and the interchange of such values with other neighbouring kingdoms over five centuries. The Historic Monuments and Sites in Kaesong are exceptional testimony to the unified Goryeo civilization as Buddhism gave way to neo-Confucianism in East Asia. The site meets the test of authenticity and integrity with adequate conservation and management conditions.

Kaesong Historic Areas is composed of 12 separate elements. Manwoldae Palace, Goryeo Cheomseongdae Observatory, Kaesong Walls and the South Great Gate of Kaesong City Walls are properties which illustrate the ruling basis of the Goryeo Dynasty and the defensive system of the city. Songgyungwan (a former high state education institute which educated Goryeo national officials), Sungyang Sowon (a Confucian private school), Sonjuk Bridge (where Jeong Mongju, the minister of Goryeo was assassinated) and Phyochung Monuments (two stelae commemorating Jeong Mongju) are evidence of the philosophical and ideological values from the time when the ruling ideology shifted from Buddhism to Confucianism. Tomb of King Wang Kon, the Seven Tombs Cluster and Myongrung Tomb, and the Tomb of King Kongmin are elements displaying the authority and continuity of the Goryeo Dynasty.

In order to protect the Kaesong Historic Areas from excessive developmental pressures, the North Korean Government has prepared new management plans and guidelines for the heritage. The natural elements within the buffer zone such as the mountains and forestry, together with the traditional housing district are also included in the management plan.

500 years of history left in ruins - Manwoldae and the Kaesong City Walls

The current city layout of Kaesong was accomplished in the Goryeo Dynasty. The palace, palace walls and outer walls were established during the early years of Goryeo as the political and administrative center as well as the residence of the king. In the later years of the dynasty the 4-fold layers of the fortress walls including the outer city walls were constructed, completing the capital city defense system.

Manwoldae sits on the southern foot of Mount Songak, the main guardian mountain of Kaesong. It is on the site of the house of Wang Kon (877~943) who was the founder and first king of Goryeo. According to pungsu principles it was

Site of Manwoldae Palace

Embankment and stairways(Manwoldae Palace Site)

recognized as an auspicious site where a king will be born to establish a new state.

High terraces were built like stairs on the steep slope, and hundreds of palace buildings were placed on top of the terraces. This is a rare style to be found in the palace architecture of East Asia. The main hall Hoegyeongjeon area demonstrates the highly esteemed authority of the emperor. The engineering and architectural skills of the Goryeo people can be clearly seen through Manwoldae.

The city walls of Kaesong has multiple layers, the palace walls protecting the palace, the imperial walls surrounding

Trial Excavation on Site of Manwoldae Palace

these areas, with outer walls (Naseong and Oeseong) added to the exterior. Naeseong, also called Banwolseong, had 2,600 kans going around with 20 gates. The Naseong outer walls surround the entire city of Kaesong and stretched almost 16km. Throughout the 500 year history, fortress walls were added to the existing structures in order to defend the dynasty from external invasions from China, Japan and the Mongols. Currently the fortress walls partially remain together with the South Great Gate.

The palace name Manwoldae was given during the Joseon Dynasty after the fall of Goryeo. It refers to a high pavilion where the full moon can be enjoyed. The ruins of the palace of a preceding dynasty were sentimentally viewed by the descendants. Gil Jae (吉再, 1353 ~ 1419) a renowned Confucian scholar who witnessed the demise of Goryeo composed a poem lamenting the ruins of the palace which was once the scene of glorious history.

Entering the five hundred year capital alone on a horse

Mountains and rivers remain as they were, but the gifted of the past are nowhere to be seen

Alas! Glorious days of the past all seem but a dream.

North Korea and South Korea are collaborating on the excavation of Manwoldae since 2007. The palace grounds are extensive and it is not possible to estimate how long the excavations will continue. There are high hopes that the ongoing excavations and research will be able to reveal the magnificent culture of the Goryeo Dynasty.

A mysterious structure - Goryeo Cheomseongdae (Observatory)

Both in the East and West astronomy, the study of stars and the universe has been an important academic field to humanity. Astronomy played an important role in deciding the destiny of a state during the ancient and medieval times of history.

As there was a Cheomseongdae (Observatory) in the Silla capital of Gyeongju, it has been conjectured that there would have been an observatory to study the stars even in the Goryeo Dynasty. Records from the period such as the chapters of Astronomy, Calender, Offices (sub chapter Seoungwan) written in 『*Goryeosa* (History of Goryeo)』 also confirm that stars were studied during Goryeo, together with the existence of an observatory.

A stone structure stands to the west of the palace site in Kaesong. It is sqaure-shaped overall, with 3m long rectangular stone pieces supporting all four corners and the center. Rectangular stone rafts 3m long are placed on top of the stone pillars.

Kaesong Cheomseongdae Observatory

This frame has been historically known as Cheomseongdae, and judging from the form and structure it is highly possible that this is the observatory dating from the Goryeo Dynasty. However as there are no mention of Cheomseongdae in ancient records with the lack of precise observation records of stars, it is difficult to know how the Goryeo people studied the stars from this structure and what they used for such observations. It is therefore difficult to confirm the conclusion that this structure is indeed the Cheomseongdae of Goryeo. There are still many unanswered questions as to the true nature of the Goryeo Cheomseongdae which need to be addressed through scientific research and investigations.

The symbol of the Goryeo Dynasty authority - Mausoleum of King Wang Kon, Seven Tombs Cluster, Myongrung, and the Mausoleum of King Kongmin

Many of the Goryeo royal tombs are located around the city of Kaesong. However they were looted and damaged considerably over the times, especially during the Japanese Colonial Period and the Korean War. A number of the tombs still need to be investigated in detail to identify the occupants. Three royal tombs belonging to the 6th King Seongjong (tomb name Gangneung), 11th King Munjong (tomb name Gyeongneung), and 12th King Sunjong (Seongneung) are situated in Panmungun

Tomb of King Kongmin (Hyeonjeongneung Royal Tomb)

County near the Military Demarcation Line. When the Mongols invaded Goryeo in the 13th century, Goryeo had to relocate the capital from Kaesong to Ganghwa Island for 39 years. Four tombs constructed during this period still exist in Ganghwado Island in South Korea. The royal tombs of Goryeo included in the World Heritage Historic Monuments and Sites in Kaesong are the Mausoleum of King Wang Kon, Seven Tombs Cluster, Myongrung Tomb and the Mausoleum of King Kongmin.

The Mausoleum of King Wang Kon (tomb name Hyeolleung),

tomb of the founding father of Goryeo, underwent a large scale refurbishment by the North Korean government in 1994. The occupants of the seven tombs are unidentified as they were looted by the Japanese colonial rule. Myongrung belongs to King Chungmok who was throned at the age of 8 and died when he was 12 years old. There are two more royal tombs in the vicinity of Myongrung, but the occupants of the tombs still remain to be clarified as the tombs are greatly damaged from past lootings.

Tombs Hyeolleung and Jeongneung belonging to King Kongmin (1330-1374) and his Queen Princess Noguk (?-1365) respectively. King Kongmin married the Princess Noguk from the Yuan Dynasty of China and carried out political reformations of Goryeo. However the queen died in 1365 due to complications of childbirth of their first child, and the King grieved over her death. He abandoned everything and concentrated on building the most splendid tomb for his queen. Once the tomb was completed, the King resorted to alcohol and the comforts of women, and eventually was brutally assassinated by one of his attendants. Goryeo rapidly collapsed after the death of King Kongmin.

The mausoleum of King Kongmin is a masterpiece encompassing all the knowledge and techniques of Goryeo in areas of mathematics, astronomy, stone masonry and sculptural arts. A unique feature of the tombs is the existence of a small corridor connecting the two stone chambers, intended to be the path for the spirits to go back and forth. It appears that the king and queen wished to continue their love even after death.

The royal tombs of Goryeo are stone chamber tombs inheriting the traditions of Goguryeo and Silla. The tomb murals (Four Cardinal Deities, figures and daily scenes, 12 zodiacs) are influences from Goguryeo, whilst the mound construction shows Silla traits. The unique features of Goryeo is represented by the new structures and stone objects adorning the tombs such as the stone pillar, stone lantern and the Jeong (丁) shaped shrine. These features were passed on to the tomb layout of Joseon.

Blood shed by the last loyal patron of Goryeo - Seonjuk Bridge, Phyochung Monuments and Sungyang Sowon

There are three sites in Kaesong related to Jeong Mongju (1337~1392), the patron and official of Goryeo known for his loyalty and integrity. Seonjuk Bridge is where his last blood was shed, Phyochung monuments were erected in commemoration of his integrity, and Sungyang Sowon, a Confucian academy and shrine was established on the site of his house.

Jeong Mongju was the last loyal patron of the dwindling Goryeo Dynasty in its last days, striving to revive the country by pursuing reforms together with Jeong Dojeon and Yi Seonggye (the founder of Joseon). However whilst Jeong Dojeon and Yi Seonggye were revolutionary, wishing to overthrow Goryeo to build a new Dynasty, Jeong Mongju never gave up hope to

Seonjuk Bridge

revive Goryeo Dynasty. In consequence he was assassinated with a mace by Yi Bangwon (son of Yi Seonggye and later King Taejong of Joseon) and his men on Seonjuk Bridge and Goryeo was soon overthrown. On the night that Jeong Mongju was killed on the bridge, it is said that bamboo trees which are symbols of loyalty and integrity sprung up from beside the bridge, which gave the bridge its new name of Seonjuk Bridge. The blood shed by Jeong Mongju left marks on the bridge which apparently still exists.

Seongjuk Bridge (No. 159 of the DPRK National Treasure) is a stone bridge near the South Gate of Kaesong City measuring 8.35m in length and 3.36m in width.

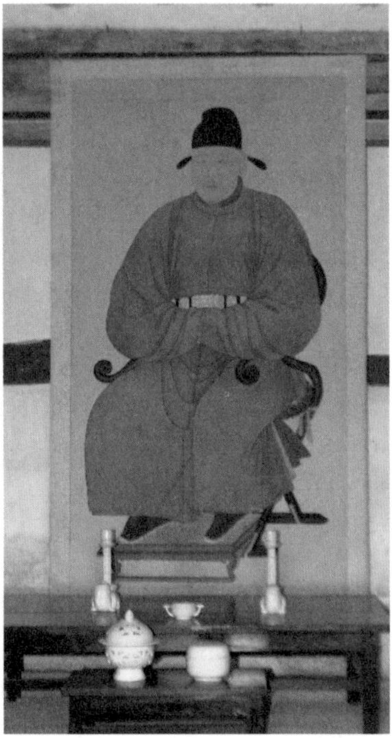

Portrait of Jeong Mongju(Sungyang Sowon)

On the other side of the bridge there are two stone monuments erected later by the Joseon Kings Yeongjo (1740) and Gojong (1872) in commemoration of Jeong Mongju. The turtle supporting the stele is intricately sculptured

Sungyang Sowon

and the stele is made of black marble stone. These are representative monuments showing the techniques of Joseon Dynasty sculpture.

Sungyang Sowon was established in the site of Jeong Mongju's house in 1573 by Confucian scholars from the regions of Kaesong, commemorating Jeong Mongju and Seo Gyeongdeok(1489~1546), a Joseon Dynasty Confucian scholar. Sowon were widely founded in Joseon to rear Confucian students.

Phyochung Monument and its explanation panel

Jeong Mongju was killed for opposing against the new dynasty of Joseon in showing his allegiance to the withering kingdom of Goryeo. Ironically though, he became the symbol of loyalty and integrity during the Joseon Dynasty. It was probably a way to soothe the public minds grieving the loss of a great politician and scholar.

The poem that Jeong wrote and recited to the son of Yi Bangwon just before he died, distinctly shows his stance and position.

Though I die and die again a hundred times,

That my bones turn to dust, whether my soul remains or not,

Ever loyal to my Lord, how can this red heart ever fade away?

The beginning of a new Confucian nation - Kaesong Songgyungwan

Kaesong Songgyungwan Confucian Academy is the highest ranking educational academy of the Goryeo Dynasty which is located in Bangjik-dong of Kaesong City. It was built in 992 and is currently designated as National Treasure No. 127 of the DPRK. The term "Songgyun" means to "mature a person and rectify the customs" and the name was given to the academy in 1310. The current structure was restored in 1602, when

Kaesong Songgyungwan

Kaesong Songgyungwan(Kaesong Goryeo History Museum)

the original building burnt down in 1592 during the Japanese invasions.

Approximately ten buildings including the lecture hall Myeongryundang, Daeseongjeon, the shrine of Confucius and related facilities compose the academy compound, together with a 500 year old ginkgo tree (Natural Monument No. 386 of the DPRK) symbolizing Confucianism. The buildings are simple yet austere, built in accordance to Confucian principles.

Ever since the introduction of Buddhism, from the Three Kingdoms period to the end of Goryeo Dynasty the countries that occupied this land based its ruling ideology on Buddhism. The religion had immense influence on all aspects of society, politics and culture. However by the end of the Goryeo Dynasty, both the Buddhist sect and the royal family lost the authority and faith of the people due to immorality and corruptness. A new group of officials armed with Confucian principles who studied at the Songgyungwan became the leaders of the reformation. The reformist politician Jeong Mongju was also a graduate of Songgyungwan, who became the principal of Songgyungwan in 1375, greatly reviving the wave of Confucianism in Goryeo. It was in the midst of such reformation that the Buddhist nation Goryeo collapsed and the Confucian nation Joseon was established.

After the foundation of Joseon, a new Seonggyungwan was built in 1398 in the capital city of Hanyang (present day Seoul). Thus Joseon now had two Seonggyungwan academies. The one in Kaesong was lowered one step in stature as a regional school Hyanggyo, but still maintained its name of Songgyungwan.

Songgyungwan in Kaesong still carries on the tradition as a university in North Korea called Goryeo Songgyungwan, and the new Seonggyungwan in Seoul has been succeeded by Sungkyunkwan University. The two schools have established sister relations in 1998 in respect of their shared historic backgrounds that have been maintained for over 1,000 years.

From 1998, parts of the Kaesong Songgyungwan has been renovated and used as the Kaesong Goryeo History Museum, housing about 10,000 relics. However according to the ICOMOS evaluations, the North Korean government is planning to build a new museum and restore the original form of Songgyungwan by 2015.

More Information

「*Goryeosa*」

「*Goryeosa Dogyeong*」

「*Encyclopedia of Korea Culture*」

National Research Institute of Cultural Heritage, *Cultural Heritage of Kaesong*, 2013

www.k-heritage.tv

Names of places and heritage follows the romanization provided in the nomination of the World Heritage Kaesong Historic Areas from the Democratic People's Republic of Korea (North Korea). Other historic terms such as the names of kings or names of historic dynasties follow the romanization of the Republic of Korea (South Korea).

Housing the spirit of Joseon

Jongmyo Shrine

Jeoung Myoung Sik(Cultural Heritage Administration)

Jongmyo, housing the spirits of Joseon

600 years ago, when Hanyang was selected as the capital city of the new state of Joseon, the founding father King Taejo first built Jongmyo Shrine in the east and Sajikdan Altar in the west. Gyeongbokgung Palace was placed in between the two. Jongmyo is a shrine to house the spiritual tablets of the kings and queens of Joseon and to perform rituals. It was important for the king to sincerely conduct ancestral rituals as a way of practicing the national philosophy of Confucianism. Therefore the shrine to hold and to revere the ancestral kings' spiritual tablets was the most esteemed place of the state. The original structure of Jongmyo has been preserved from the 16th century, and has been marked as a unique ritual place worldwide.

'It's hard to find such an impressive space as Jongmyo Jeongjeon.'

- Frank Gehry, Canadian-American architect

Jeongjeon Hall is the most solemn and sacred building in which the spiritual tablets of the kings and queens are kept and the rituals take place. Everytime a king's tablet was added, the building was lengthened room by room. The 19 rooms make Jeongjeon the longest single building in the world. As the philosophical background of Joseon, Confucianism emphasized the importance of filial piety and ancestral worship. Therefore Jongmyo displays forbearance and solemnity with restrained design and form.

Only the front side of the building has wooden doors and

windows whilst all the other three sides are closed up with brick walls. It is intended to provide the ancestral spirits with peaceful rest. The dark interior not allowing a stream of light is the place for the dead, whilst the exterior full of light is the space for the living.

The space reserved for the dead is absolutely dark and still. Ritual day is the day when the spirits are exposed to the living world emerging from the dark and stillness. The living lift up the latches and open the heavy doors to reach the spiritual space.

Jongmyo ancestral ritual is composed of services, ritual vessels, instrumental music, songs and dance. It was formulated in 1462 during the reign of King Sejong, which has been inherited for over 500 years up to this day. It is possibly the

Jongmyo

Jungyeonji Pond. The rectangular outline of the pond represents the earth and the round island in the middle represents the heavens. It is also called the Bangjiwondo.

Mangmyoru, a place to think of the predecessors and the state

Shrine of King Gongmin, where the portraits of the Goryeo Dynasty King Gongmin and his queen are kept.

Jaegung is located at the southeastern side of the Jeongjeon (main hall) of Jongmyo where the king and the crown prince stayed to prepare for the ritual. The king and the prince would cleanse their body and soul here, dress in clean clothes and would proceed to uphold the ritual by exiting the west sidegate of Jaegung and entering into the east gate of Jeongjeon

Eojaesil, a place where the king stayed

Sejajaesil, a room for the crown prince to stay in

Eomogyokcheong (Royal bath), where the king cleansed his body

Jeonsacheong, a place to prepare the the ritual food

Hyangdaecheong, a place to keep the ritual goods and equipment, which was used as a preparation room by the ritual officiants

Jejeong, the well used for the ritual which does not dry up even during a drought

Jeongjeon, a place with solemn and elegant corridor, houses the spiritual tablets of the kings and queens of Joseon.

How often were Jongmyo Jerye ancestral rituals conducted?

During the Joseon Dynasty there were regular rituals and intermittent rituals. Regular rituals were held at the first month of spring, summer, autumn and winter in January, April, July and October whilst intermittent rituals were conducted when good or bad events happened in the country. Currently the ritual is only held once a year on the first Sunday of May, but the formalities, order and procedures of the ritual are strictly upheld and solemnly conducted. .

oldest comprehensive ritual culture in the world which has been protected in its original form.

The spiritual tablets of the kings originally housed in Jeongjeon were moved to Yeongnyeongjeon after five generations passed by. However kings highly esteemed for their great accomplishments like King Sejong were kept housed in Jeongjeon even after five generations.

To which side were the shrines expanded?

Counting only the spritual rooms, Jeongjeon which started out with 7 kans was expanded three times, with 4 kans added at each occasion, finally totaling 19 kans. King Taejo, the first king is housed in the western-most room and the descending kings go eastwards. It follows the rule of acknowledging the west as superior to the east. As it was considered inappropriate to move the most important tablets housed in the west side of the shrine, the expansion took place on the eastern end of the building.

Extension of Jeongjeon and Yeongnyeongjeon

Many architectural structures were burnt down in Joseon due

Rituals were conducted in the hour of 'chuk' (one o'clock in the morning) during the Joseon Dynasty. It was a tiring task to get ready and wait for the ritual time. A waiting room for the king called the Jaegung Eosuksa was prepared in Jongmyo. The Confucian tradition of conducting ancestral rituals is still carried on in Korea these days. However social custom has evolved into a form where all the greater family members return to their houses after the ritual. Therefore it is now more common to conduct the ritual around 9 to 10pm.

to the frequent invasions of foreign forces. This was also the same for Jongmyo. Jeongjeon which started out as a 7-kan (a unit of space between pillars) structure was expanded to 11 kan in 1546 but was burnt down during the Seven Years War against Japan in 1592. Right after the war ended, Jeongjeon was rebuilt as a 11-kan structure in 1608, expanded once in 1726 as a 15-kan structure, and was finally finished as a 19-kan structure in 1836. Spiritual tablets of 49 kings and queens are currently housed inside the building.

Yeongnyeongjeon was newly built in 1421 as a 6-kan structure when there were too many tablets to be kept in Jeongjeon. It also burnt down during the Seven Years War (1592) and was rebuilt as a 10-kan structure in 1608. Expanded as a 12-kan structure in 1667 and to 16-kans in 1836, there are tablets for 34 kings and queens housed inside.

Jeonjeon built in brick walls with no windows on three sides shows its inaccessbility.

The black path is the 'spirit road' that leads the ancestral kings' souls to the spirit rooms.

Gongsindang, a shrine to house tablets of subjects who contributed meritorious services to the state.

Chilsadang, a shrine to worship the seven gods of the folk beliefs.

Akgongcheong, a space for the ritual musicians

The roughly trimmed arch-stones fill the woldae (elevated platform), which is the largest woldae in Korea measuring 109m x 69m. The arch-stones made of granite is strong and rough which is the most commonly found rock type, familiar to every Korean. Almost all the stone heritage in Korea is manufactured of granite.

Why are there 35 king's spiritual tablets in Jongmyo when there were only 27 kings in Joseon? (19 tablets in Jeongjeon and 16 tablets in Yeongnyeongjeon)

There are posthumous kings in Joseon who were honored as kings after death. One example is King Jangjo, who died when he was Crown Prince Sado. There are a total of 35 spiritual tablets housed in Jongmyo, with 9 posthumous kings, and Crown Prince Euimin, the last prince of Joseon. However the two kings who were dethroned during their reigns (Yeonsangun and Gwanghaegun) are excluded from Jongmyo.

Ancestral Ritual at Jongmyo

Diary of a carpenter

The state of conservation of Jongmyo is kept at a good level. Although the Joseon Dynasty came to an end in the modern era, the 'Royal Yi Family Repair Team' was formed, being responsible for the management of the palaces and Jongmyo. The current 'Conservation Team for State-designated Heritage' of the Cultural Heritage Administration stems from this team. As master carpenter I am part of the conservation team, and the team consists of specialized and certified heritage specialists who are in charge of the conservation and repairs of the World Heritage Jongmyo.

Changdeokgung Palace, the Royal Tombs of the Joseon Dynasty, and Jongmyo Shrine are my places of work and places to learn. Every work is conducted respecting traditional skills, techniques and materials to maintain the authenticity of the heritage.

Yeongnyeongjeon Hall

Tips for enjoying Jongmyo

1. As Jeongjeon was expanded many times to the right side, the staircase in the middle was also relocated. Try to find traces of the staircase side panels.
2. The roof-end tiles hanging by the tip of the roof have various patterns such as dragons, phoenices, Su (壽) character, spiders and flowers. Try to find designs from the Joseon Dynasty.
3. The sexagenary cycle is inscribed on the stone base of the outer walls of Jongmyo. The walls were refurbished in the 1930s when urbanization in the vicinity took place, and the numerical figures were inscribed at regular

Samdo, the three level path. Try to walk alongside the path together with the spirits to Jeongjeon and Yeongnyeongjeon Halls with reverence.

intervals for purpose of management. Try to locate the inscription 'rebuilt in March, 8th year of Showa' and the sexagenary figures.

4. With the natural environment well preserved, there are racoons living in Jongmyo. Try to spot one who greets the visitors every morning like the host of Jongmyo.

More Information

Royal Palaces and Jongmyo of Joseon, Cultural Heritage Administration, Nulwa, 2010.

Jongmyo Jeryeak, Ritual Music of Jongmyo, National Research Institute of Cultural Heritage, Minsokwon, 2008.

Stories of Korean Architecture, Kim Bongryol, Dolbegae, 2006.

Jongmyo and Sajik, Kim Donguk, Daewonsa, 2005.

Stories of Korean Traditional Architecture – Jongmyo, Myoungsik Jeong, Gangseo-gu District Children's Library Newspaper, 2013.

Breathing 600 years of history

Royal Tombs of the Joseon Dynasty

Jeoung Myoung Sik (Cultural Heritage Administration)

The Royal Tombs of the Joseon Dynasty are tombs of the Kings and Queens from Joseon which shows the unique funerary culture embodying the ideology, political history and artistic taste of the historic era. The spatial construction, architecture, and stone masonry of the tombs have outstanding artistry, whilst the surrounding natural environments were selected according to pungsu geomancy principles.[1] Combined with the records of the *Salleung Dogam Uigwe* (山陵都監儀軌, Records of the Office for the Royal Tombs)[2], the royal tombs are still alive and breathing as a cultural heritage where the tradition of ancestral worship has been carried on for more than 600 years. The 40

1) Pungsu principle refers to the geomantic theory of finding an ideal site in the environment. Usually an ideal site sits in an outstanding landscape with water flowing to the south and a mountain shielding the rear, with mountain ridges surrounding the site from a distance.

2) Salleung Dogam Uigwe are official records of the entire process, rituals and procedures needed for constructing a royal tomb for a king or a queen.

Joseon Royal Tombs, excluding the two located in North Korea, have been inscribed on the UNESCO World Heritage List in 2009 to be cherished by all humanity.

The stylistic development and changes of the royal tombs over a period of 600 years reflect the governing ideology and the political situations of the Joseon Dynasty (1392-1910). As the ruling ideology of Joseon was Confucianism, the royal tombs were constructed faithfully following its principles and formalities. The size, separation of areas, arrangement and details of stone sculptures and other facilities varied and changed reflecting the circumstances of each period. The ancestral rituals were carried out for 600 years, and nowadays are conducted by the Royal Family Organization of the Jeonju

Yeongjo, the 21st king of Joseon wished to be buried next to the queen consort, Jeongseong. The tomb for her was designed in twin tombs so that King Yeongjo could be buried next to her. However when Yeongjo passed away, his grandson, King Jeongjo buried him in Wonreung disobeying his grandfather's wishes.

Burial Area is the core area of Royal Tombs which is usually placed on a gentle slope. It is surrounded by low stone fence and pine trees. Mound area in the shape of circle is covered with green grass.

Yi Clan. Ancestral worship rituals practised by the descendants regardless of the demise of the dynasty is a unique feature of the Korean tradition.

Entrance Area This area was used for preparation of the ancestral rituals, where the tombkeeper stayed to manage the tombs. It is the secular area before entering into the sacred area.

Ceremonial Area The dead and the alive meet in the ceremonial area. For normal tombs, ancestral rituals are conducted right in front of the tomb mound, whereas rituals for the royal tombs take place in the ceremonial area. The T-shaped shrine is where the ritual is conducted, whilst the royal kitchen

Jaesil, the tombkeeper's house located at the entrance area of the royal tomb was used for ancestral ritual preparations.

△△ Geumcheongyo bridge, marks the boundary of the secular area for the living and the sacred area for the spirits. The bridge crossing the stream symbolizes cleansing of the body and soul before entering into the sacred burial area.
△ The flat stone dais to the right of the red spiked gate is called a panwi, upon which visitors bow deeply to the buried at the beginning and the end of the ritual.

After crossing the Geumcheongyo bridge, the red spiked gate stands to indicate the sanctity of the sacred area.

From the red spiked gate thin stone slabs are placed to form a pathway called chamdo leading up to the T-shaped shrine. The wide path in the middle is intended for the spirit of the buried king and the living king and his subjects take the lower and narrower path (eodo) on the side.

and guards' house were used for the ritual preparations.

The T-shaped shrine is the main architectural feature of the royal tombs. It is called the Jeongjagak, literally meaning the 丁(jeong)-shaped shrine. The living king and the spirit of the

Looking out from the T-shaped shrine, the royal guards' house stands to the left, which were used by those guarding the royal tombs. The royal kitchen used for preparation of ritual food stands to the right, facing the guards' house.

Ancestral rituals are conducted in the T-shaped shrine (Jeongjagak).

A stele bearing records of achievements of the buried is protected within the stele house.

The T-shaped shrine is the main architectural feature of the royal tombs. It is called the Jeongjagak, literally meaning the 丁(jeong)-shaped shrine.

A total of 53 ancestral rituals are conducted yearly for the 40 neungs and 13 wons.

The retaining stones were embossed with the twelve zodiacs or peony decorations symbolizing guardian motifs. They also functioned as protective shields preventing the sinking of the mound and the break in of harmful insects.

buried king walk down the path together from the red spiked gate reaching the T-shaped shrine by the two staircases in the east. After the ritual is finished, the spirit of the buried king goes to the burial mound beyond the shrine and the living king descends the stairs on the west side.

Sacred Area The area beyond the T-shaped shrine is the sacred burial area. Although the size is different, the symbolic composition of the burial area resembles the layout of the royal palace where the king used to live. The area consists of a burial mound and stone sculptures protecting the mound. The sacred area is usually kept closed from general visits.

Burial Area The burial mound is surrounded by various

Stone sheep and stone tigers have symbolic meanings of driving away evil spirits.

stone sculptures of people and animals which are guardians of the tomb. The stone statues of the civil and military officials, stone animals and the stone guard rails show the artistic quality

The stone statues signify the official subjects of the king. Regulations for setting up stone statues and figures were established in 1474 during the reign of King Seongjong.

Yegam is a square stone case used for burning the prayer paper after rituals.

Stone pillars were erected in order to identify the tomb from far away and to guide the spirit to find its way to the tomb.

The stone dais in front of the mound is not for laying down ritual food, but is a platform for the spirits to rest or play.

Stone horses symbolize the transportation means of the civil and military officials.

The curved walls surrounding the tomb mound are meant to protect the tomb from hostile winds blowing into the tomb.

and the periodic styles. According to each period the shapes and forms of the clothes on the stone officials change, whilst the diverse size and facial expressions reflect the political, economic situations of the particular times when the statues were manufactured. The royal tombs of the Joseon Dynasty are extraordinary places to read the history of 600 years, where the humorous expressions and depictions can also be enjoyed.

Tips for enjoying the Royal Tombs of the Joseon Dynasty

1. The burial areas of most of the tombs are closed for general visits due to conservation purposes. However the burial areas of Myeongreung inside the Seooreung Cluster in Goyang City and Mokreung in Donggureung Cluster are open to the public. Heolleung and Illeung in Seocho-gu District also have visitor platforms to ensure close up viewing of the burial areas. Here you can get a detailed view of the burial mound and the various stone sculptures.
2. Looking out from the T-shaped shrine, there are two staircases to the right, for the Spirit's road and the King's road, whereas there is only one staircase to the left, the King's road. This is because after the ritual is finished, the spirit goes back to the burial mound, and only the living King comes down the staircase to the left. Imagine yourself as the officiator of the ancestral ritual and try to follow the path from the entrance area of the tomb.
3. There are various different types of burial mounds. There are double

mounds where the king and queen are buried side by side, or three consecutive mounds where the first and second queens were buried together with the king. There are also cases where two mounds are distanced in a different hill although sharing the same T-shaped shrine. Sometimes the king and queen were buried together in one mound, or at times they were completely separated and buried in entirely different places. Their destiny was determined by the next king. The fate of the dead and alive kept changing hands for 600 years throughout the entire dynasty. The history of the entire period of Joseon can be read from the burial mounds and information boards on site.

More Information

Royal Palaces and Jongmyo of Joseon, Cultural Heritage Administration, Nulwa, 2010.

Visiting Guidebook to the Royal Tombs of the Joseon Dynasty, Cultural Heritage Administration, Misul Munhwa, 2012.

UNESCO World Heritage from School Textbooks, Lee Hyungjun, Sigong Junior, 2011.

Cultural Heritage Administration Website www.cha.go.kr

Seooreung Website http://goyang.cha.go.kr

Donggureung Website http://donggu.cha.go.kr/n_donggu/index.html

UNESCO World Heritage, Korean National Commission for UNESCO Website http://www.unesco.or.kr/heritage

Delivering the teachings of the Buddha

Haeinsa Temple Janggyeong Panjeon, Depositories for the *Tripitaka Koreana* Woodblocks

Lee Hyun Sung (A&A Research Institute of Culture)

The Dharma Temple Haeinsa of the Three Jewel Temples

Haeinsa Temple is known as one of the Three Jewel Temples of Korea together with Tongdosa and Songgwangsa Temples. The three jewels refer to the Buddha, the Dharma (teachings of the Buddha) and the Sangha (community of monks who deliver the Buddha's teachings). As Haeinsa houses the wooden blocks of the Tripitaka Koreana, the teachings of the Buddha, it is known as the Dharma temple. The preservation of the *Tripitaka Koreana* woodblocks was made possible because of the Janggyeong Panjeon, the depository buildings. The other two jewel temples are Tongdosa of Yangsan, in which the sarira of the Buddha is housed, therefore known as the Buddha Temple, and Songgwangsa in Suncheon from which arose 15 great

View of Haeinsa Temple (Catalogue of Historic Sites in Joseon)

monks since the Goryeo Dynasty, thus known as the Sangha Temple.

The *Tripitaka Koreana* woodblocks were produced during the Mongol invasions in the Goryeo Dynasty, whilst the depositories were built in the early Joseon Dynasty. An entry in 『*Samguk Sagi* (Chronicles of the Three Kingdoms)』 records that 'Haeinsa of Gayasan Mountain was founded' in August of the 3rd year of King Aejangwang's reign, which is 802 CE during the

Unified Silla period. As a representative temple of the Hwaeom Sect, the name of the temple was derived from a verse in the Avatamsaka Sutra '*haein sammae*', the state of samadhi reached when the Buddha was preaching the Avatamsaka Sutra. Samadhi is the state of consciousness induced by complete meditation as a practice in Buddhism and refers to a state in which everything in this world is visible to the mind as if it was being reflected in the ocean. The name was probably chosen to wish that all the people who came to the temple may reach a clear and tranquil state of mind as can be shown in the vast ocean.

Exclusiveness of the building being designed to store the Tripitaka Woodblocks

There are two UNESCO enlisted heritage in Haeinsa Temple. The printing woodblocks of the *Tripitaka Koreana* and miscellaneous Buddhist scriptures were inscribed on the Memory of the World register in 2007, and the Janggyeong Panjeon, the depositories were inscribed on the World Heritage List earlier in 1995. The full name of the World Heritage property is "Haeinsa Temple Janggyeong Panjeon, the Depositories for the *Tripitaka Koreana* Woodblocks". The depositories are considered unique both in terms of their antiquity so far as this specialized type of structure is concerned, and also for the remarkably effective solutions developed in the 15th century to address the problem of storing and conserving the 80,000 woodblocks against deterioration, which were used for printing Buddhist scriptures. Also the Janggyeong Panjeon and its unique collection of 13th century *Tripitaka Koreana* woodblocks, outstanding for their artistry and excellent execution of engraving techniques, occupy an exceptional position in the history of Buddhism as the most complete and accurate corpus of Buddhist doctrinal texts in the world. These were the reasons for its inscription on the World Heritage List.

The depositories were built in 1488 and it is an exclusive case worldwide to be built as a storage house solely to protect woodblocks. They are also the oldest buildings remaining in Haeinsa Temple. Although the temple was established in the Unified Silla period, it witnessed many fires and especially in the late Joseon Dynasty, a majority of the buildings

Center three-storied stupa

Past and present of the Janggyeong Panjeon

were burnt down. However the depositories are the only buildings which have been kept intact preserving its original form. This is due to the fact that it was distanced away from the rest of the temple to ensure the protection of the woodblocks. Located on a much higher ground and surrounded with walls closing off the area from other parts of the temple, measures were already taken to prevent the possible damage from fire.

The Janggyeong Panjeon consists of four separate buildings. Originally there were only two buildings, Beopbojeon (Hall of Dharma Jewel) to the north and Sudarajang Hall (Storage of Sutra) to the south. However in later years the two smaller annex buildings were added to the east and west completing a rectangular layout with a courtyard in the middle. All four buildings have columns with entasis leaning inwards, with

Daejeokgwangjeon Hall (Hall of Great Silence and Light) of Haeinsa Temple

the end columns slightly raised higher than the others. The buildings are generally simple and modest.

Looking closer, the Beopbojeon and Sudarajang are erected on platforms not too high with the columns being supported with naturally shaped base stones. They have wing-shaped brackets with five-cross beam structure, single lined eaves and a lotus-type ceiling. High columns are placed in the inner center of the buildings. The regular columns have a slight entasis, whilst the center higher columns are cornered. The east and west annex buildings also have wing-shaped brackets with three-cross beam structure and a gabled roof. The ceilings are also lotus-type ceilings.

View of the Janggyeong Panjeon Depositories

West annex building

The essence of wisdom - the window bars and floors of the Janggyeong Panjeon

The Janggyeong Panjeon appears humble and unassuming unlike the luxuriously painted Daejeokgwangjeon Hall housing the Vairocana Buddha or Daebirojeon Hall. Both Beopbojeon and Sudarajang Halls of the depositories housing the woodblocks are simple and austere. The buildings appear to be ordinary wooden structures with lime plastered walls on the exterior. However the wisdom of our ancestral architects is hidden within the buildings which ensured the near perfect preservation of the woodblocks.

The woodblocks stored inside the Janggyeong Panjeon.

Out of the ordinary features, the first element of wisdom is shown in the numerous windows with wooden bars. These show the unique window structures of the building for the effective protection of the woodblocks. The two buildings have windows all around, but the sizes of the windows are different depending on their location and direction. The southern wall has larger windows on the bottom and smaller windows on the top, whilst the northern wall has larger windows placed on top and smaller ones at the bottom. When the sun rises, the dry and warm wind flow into the buildings through the large bottom row windows and exit through the northern top row windows. The dry and warm wind brings out the humidity of the building which aids in protecting the original form of the woodblocks.

The shelves are also placed in a sequence to steadily maintain the temperature and humidity by controlling the flow of natural air. The length of the roof eaves are designed so that the sunlight does not reach the woodblocks directly.

The wisdom of the ancestors are hidden underground as well. Before the buildings were built, the grounds were dug out deeply and filled up with charcoal, salt, and lime powder mixed with sand and clay. Charcoal, salt and lime powder are effective for absorbing moisture. These materials collect the existing moisture during the wet season and emit it out again during the dry winter seasons, ensuring the constant moisture level inside the depositories. Such scientific planning of the buildings have proved their effectiveness by the intact woodblocks having been preserved for more than 600 years. The depositories are significant features in the advance of technology.

Different sizes of the windows on the top and bottom.

Tips for enjoying Haeinsa

Why are the Tripitaka Koreana called the Palman Daejanggyeong (80,000 Daejanggyeong)?

The Tripitaka Koreana woodblocks of the Goryeo Dynasty are commonly called the Palman Daejanggyeong (the 80,000 woodblocks). There are two reasons how the name was derived. First it has been known that the number 84000 was used as a number indicating innumerable quantity in India, which gave its name to the woodblocks which had immeasurable numbers of blocks. The other originates from the 84,000 Dharma of Buddha, which are teachings for each afflictions of the human mind. As the woodblocks are manuscripts of the Dharma, it is called the Palman (80,000) Daejanggyeong, indicating the number of teachings of the Buddha. It is of greater interest that there are actually 81,340 panels of woodblocks, corresponding to the two significant meanings.

Monks of Haeinsa guarding the nation in times of trouble

Buddhism played an important role in drawing together the minds of the people when the nation was facing trouble. The Tripitaka woodblocks were made when the Qitan and Mongols invaded the country, and the religion also stood up against the invasions of Japan in the 16th century and during the Japanese Colonial Period. Great Monk Samyeong fought in many battles during the Japanese Invasions of 1592, and in 1604 he was dispatched to Japan on behalf of the king, bearing King Seonjo's personal letter. He negotiated directly with Tokugawa Ieyasu of Japan and succeeded in bringing back 3,500 prisoners of war to Korea. His merits were highly noted in Joseon and he was rewarded a small temple called Hongjeam to the west of Haeinsa. The monk stupa of Samyeong stands in Hongjeam and is designated as a Treasure.

One of the leaders of the March 1st Independence Movement in 1919 was Monk Baek Yongseong, who resided in Yongtap Meditation Hall of Haeinsa. He was one of the national leaders who wrote many books to enlighten the general public, and translated Buddhist texts into Korean. He twice sent official written protests to the Resident-General Saito Makoto, criticizing the colonial religion policy. He was also a monk of practice, who believed that Buddhist temples had to become economically self supportive and must carry out both religious practice and agriculture.

More Information

Haeinsa Temple, Yi Jaechang, Jang Kyungho, Jang Chungsik, Daewonsa, 2006.

World Cultural Heritage of Korea I, Song Myeongseok, Park Jaeho, Kim Eunju, Banseok Publishers, 2013.

UNESCO World Heritage in Korea, Jeju National Museum, Seogyeong, 2007.

Survey Report of Haeinsa Janggyeong Panjeon, Yetteo Architectural Office, Cultural Heritage Administration, 2002.

Haeinsa Temple website http://www.haeinsa.or.kr/home.html

The essence of Joseon palaces

Changdeokgung Palace Complex

Lee Ji Eun (Seoul National Univ.)

Changdeokgung, the epitome of Joseon royal palaces

Taejong, the 3rd King of Joseon finished the establishment of Changdeokgung in 1405, as a new secondary palace to the official palace Gyeongbokgung. Although Gyeongbokgung

Injeongjeon Hall

If there were eastern palaces, were there northern, western and southern palaces?

There were eastern, western, and northern palaces in the capital city of Hanyang during the Joseon Dynasty. Gyeongbokgung as the official seat of the throne was called the Northern Palace, whilst Changdeokgung and Changgyeonggung Palaces were grouped as the Eastern Palaces. Gyeonghuigung Palace near the Sajikdan (Altar for the Deities of Earth and Grain) was called the Western Palace. However there was no palace which was known as the southern palace.

was the official seat of the throne, the royal family preferred to live in Changdeokgung due to pungsu reasons. Thus Changdeokgung became the center of the royal household. This is why Changdeokgung was the first palace to be restored in the early 1600s after being burnt down during the Seven Years War against Japan. In contrast it was only in 1867 that Gyeongbokgung was completely rebuilt for the royal family to move into again. However the royal family came back to reside in Changdeokgung during the reign of the last monarch Emperor Sunjong, and the palace once again restored its status as the official residence of the king.

Grouped together with the neighboring Changgyeonggung Palace, the whole compound was called the Eastern Palaces as it was located to the east of Gyeongbokgung Palace. Over 2/3 of the entire compound was destroyed during the Japanese

Elevated grounds to the south of Injeongjeon Hall

Colonial Period, and at one point Changgyeonggung Palace was degraded into an amusement park.

Inspiration within regulations

The most notable feature of Changdeokgung is the difference it displays in the arrangement of the buildings compared to other palaces. Palaces generally have a vertical axis by which the most important buildings are placed from north to south, and the buildings sit facing south. This is to display the authority of the king and the royal family through spatial arrangements. Gyeongbokgung Palace is a model example, and even today one can feel the power of space when walking around the various quarters of Gyeongbokgung.

However Changdeokgung deviates from the linear display of buildings and employs a more spontaneous layout. For example, to reach the main throne hall Injeongjeon from the main gate of Donhwamun, one has to make two right angle turns, as compared to the straight approach to reach Geunjeongjeon Main Hall from Gwanghwamun Gate in Gyeongbokgung. This is because the ground is slightly elevated to the south of Injeongjeon Hall. Rather than leveling out the ground, the designers of Changdeokgung diverged the path by placing the main gate to the west.

The principal aim was to place the main hall beneath Eungbong Peak and to conveniently place the other buildings around it, and efforts to conform to nature are cleverly disguised rather than being flaunted. The greatest appeal of Changdeokgung Palace can be found in the gardens of the palace. The natural terrain

Buyongji Pond and Juhapru Pavilion in the Gardens of Changdeokgung.

was respected as much as possible when placing structures. Thus the natural environment and architectural features are in accordance with each other to the utmost, being praised as the best architectural arrangement of the Joseon Dynasty.

There are various types of architecture inside Changdeokgung Palace spanning from the early 15th century to the early 20th century. The Geumcheongyo Bridge inside Donhwamun Gate retains its original stone structure since it was built in the early 15th century.

Donhwamun Gate (rebuilt in 1609) and Seonjeongjeon Hall (rebuilt in 1647) show the architectural style of the 17th century. Seonjeongjeon especially stands out even from a distance, as

Jondeokjeong Pavilion with the characteristic half-moon shaped roof

Geumcheongyo Bridge, the bridge from the earliest days of the palace

it is the only palace building adorned with blue roof tiles. Huijeongdang Hall (built in 1920) was built using the materials dismantled from Gangnyeongjeon Hall of Gyeongbokgung. It was used as a parlor of the king with western style chairs and a desk. A touch of the modern era can be found in the front of the building where the entrance was widened to allow motor vehicles to reach the building.

Guarding the last days of the Daehan Empire

At the beginning of the 20th century modern facilities were installed in Changdeokgung Palace such as radiators, modern kitchen installments and bathrooms for the benefit of the

Entrance of Huijeongdang Hall with a motor vehicle path

Various shapes of window frames in Huijeongdang Hall

Interior of Huijeongdang Hall

Electric lighting installments on the ceiling of Injeongjeon Hall

Nakseonjae

Support base for the stone sculpture in front of Yeongyeongdang in the gardens of Changdeokgung

Daejojeon Hall

emperor and his household.

The second emperor to reign next to Gojong was Sunjong, who moved his residence to Changdeokgung Palace from Gyeongungung (today's Deoksugung Palace) on 13th November 1907. He later died in Daejojeon Hall marking the end of the Daehan Empire and thus the end of the Joseon Dynasty.

Throughout the Japanese Colonial Period and even into the era of the Korean Republic, the former royal family members of the Daehan Empire lived in Changdeokgung Palace. In the quarters of Nakseonjae, Seokbokheon and Sugangjae in the east side of the palace lived the last crown prince Yeongchinwang (residence 1963~1970), his wife the crown princess (residence

1963~1989), and Princess Deokhye (residence 1962~1989).

UNESCO World Heritage

Changdeokgung greatly influenced the development of Joseon Dynasty palace architecture. The unique arrangement of buildings and gardens in concordance with nature based on the principles of pungsu and Confucianism was considered outstanding and earned inscription on the World Heritage List in 1997. Over the course of 500 years there had been many fires, repairs and reconstructions, but efforts to maintain the authenticity were made, and through this process the traditional architecture of Korea evolved and developed. The authenticity of such architecture and the original layout of the buildings in full respect of the natural geographical terrain shows the epitome of East Asian palace architecture and garden planning which is recognized by the world.

Donggwoldo (Painting of the Eastern Palaces), a 19th century architectural blueprint

Crown Prince Hyomyeong is known to be the producer of the Painting of the Eastern Palaces. The painting depicts the eastern palaces of the 1820~30s from a bird's eye view. The entire painting measures 5.76m wide and 2.73m tall, formed of 16 foldable books. The value of the painting is exceptional due to its precise details of the buildings and layout of the 19th century palace.

Tips for enjoying Changdeokgung

1. The oldest palace architectural structure in Korea stands in Changdeokgung. The main gate Donhwamun has stood for more than 400 years guarding the entrance of the palace.
2. A copy of the Painting of the Eastern Palaces can be purchased from the Museum Shop inside the palace. Try to locate the buildings found in the old map.
3. The moonlight tour of Changdeokgung is an opportunity not to be missed. Entrance is limited to reservation only and although making the reservation is certainly a challenge it is truly worth trying.

More Information

To enter into Donggwol, the home of Joseon, Han Youngwoo, Yeolhwadang, 2008

Reading deep into Changdeokgung, Kim Donguk et al., Geulhangari, 2012

Stories of our palace, Hong Sunmin, Cheongnyeonsa, 1999

Emergency Capital during Joseon Dynasty

Namhansanseong

Cho Doo Won (Namhansanseong World Heritage Centre)

What is Namhansanseong?

Namhansanseong was planned as an emergency capital as well as a representative mountain fortress during the Joseon dynasty (1392-1910). It is placed on a mountainous site 25 km south-east of present capital Seoul. The earliest remains date from the 7th century, but it was rebuilt several times, notably after the second Manchu Invasion of Korea in 1636. Built and defended by Buddhist soldier-monks as well as regular soldiers from Sueocheong army corps headquarter, it embodies a synthesis of the defensive military engineering concepts of the period, drawing on Chinese and Japanese influences. Changes in the art of fortification following the introduction of firearms from the West can also be clearly seen. A permanently inhabited city that was the emergency capital over a long period, it

Aerial view of the South Outworks area.

includes inside its fortified walls evidence of various types of military, civil and religious buildings. It has become a symbol of Korean sovereignty.

Namhansanseong as a defensive structure

The system of fortifications of Namhansanseong embodies a synthesis of the art of defence in the Far East of the early 17th century. It stems from a re-examination of Chinese and Korean standards of urban fortification, and from fears aroused by new firearms from the West. Namhansanseong marks a turning point in mountain fortress design in Korea, and it went on to influence in its turn the construction of fortresses in the region.

Namhansanseong exhibits the result of interchange among Korea, China and Japan during the 16th~18th centuries in its fortress layout and architecture. The Japanese Invasion of Korea (1592~1598), the continuous invasion of Qing China (1627~1637) and the subsequent years in which Joseon recognized the suzerainty of Qing had an immense influence on all aspects of the Joseon society. These changes introduced the need to construct an emergency capital city with competent defensive capacity to preserve the stability of the King and the government. These conditions resulted in the actual design, construction, and continuous reconstruction of the fortress to suit the long term warfare and to effectively respond to the new weaponry and armaments. Construction and complementary measures taken

Aerial view of Namhansanseong seen from the east

Janggyeongsa-sinji Outwork

at Namhansanseong resulted in the systemization of Joseon's fortress theories incorporating important aspects from various Chinese military defense writings. The preceding Japanese invasion underlined the importance of constructing a defense line utilizing mountain fortresses rather than flat land city walls, which triggered the actual construction of Namhansanseong as it stands today. Based on the theories of traditional fortress architecture and city layout, Namhansanseong is based upon the important principles of city construction that are shared throughout the East Asian region, whilst employing new elements that would effectively respond to the developed warfare.

As a temporary capital where the king and the people could take shelter in times of emergency, it is the only place where both a temporary palace and a local city were constructed together. The position and location of the emergency palace takes

Aerial View of the 2nd South Outwork

advantage of the natural topography to its utmost by utilizing the scenery of mountains and the skies in the background to signify the authority of the King. The layout of the city follows the principle of "government offices in front and the markets at the rear," which are traditional methods of constructing cities in East Asia including China. However independent measures to fit the natural topography were employed here, in which the royal palace is asymmetrically arranged to the east according to topography. Within Namhansanseong, both the governing facilities of the palace and authoritative structures of shrines stand together with the local administrative offices. The entire fortress resembling the traditional Korean style adopts many variations with such modifications in the slope angle of the fortress to respond to the Japanese impact. Also structures such as outworks and grooves were concepts imported from Chinese fortresses creatively applied to the Korean natural mountainous terrain in order to maximize the defensive capacity of the fortress.

A place to see the development of fortress constrcution

Namhansanseong is an outstanding example of a mountain fortress that preserves the long standing technical history of

Yeonjubong Outwork

fortress building in the region. Throughout the history of the world, and especially in the history of Korea, many fortresses and castles were built to defend one's livelihood against an enemy force. The value of Namhansanseong lies in that the fortress developed into being a living environment from being a single defensive structure only utilized in emergencies. Maximizing the advantages of the rugged terrain and locating various facilities inside the fortress it was made possible to function both as a city and a defensive structure. Recognized for its important geographical location, the site preserves walls that have been constructed since the 7th century that generates down to the 19th century preserving the distinct features of each period, especially so in the development of warfare. The techniques employed to construct the walls and individual components

Namhansanseong Emergency Palace

Sueojangdae West Command Post

all respond to the technical development of weaponry. The fortress is preserved in its entirety with administrative, military facilities and domestic urban infrastructure that was laid out during the 17th century when over 4,000 people were moved into the fortress to support the function of the city.

Namhansanseong is comprised with multi-layers of various techniques of fortress construction, thereby showing defensive strategies that were employed in each era from the 7th century until the 19th century. Within Namhansanseong, fortress stones, platforms, and a warehouse are found which dates from the 7th century of Jujangseong Fortress, the former structure standing in place. Also, Namhansanseong demonstrates the traditional fortress architecture by utilizing the mountainous terrain of Korea with various facilities of outworks and gun batteries set up after the Second Manchu invasion of Korea introduced the use of artillery. Techniques to construct paropet using grey bricks, lime and *tung* oil were adopted from Chinese construction methods. There is a clear difference in construction methods between the fortress body constructed in 1626 and the parts that were constructed after the Second Manchu Invasion of Korea in 1636, which are the three defensive walls, five outworks, and various defensive facilities. Namhansanseong actively adopted bastions with gun-firing embrasures, shooting apertures (grooves in the fortress walls), lookouts, command posts, and others so as to confront the new and effective Dutch artillery. The 1st, 2nd and 3rd south outworks were for both attacking and defending facilities which set up to comprehensively serve as lookouts

Janggyeongsa Military Buddhist Temple

Fortress wall at 1st South Outwork

equipped with shooting apertures, outwork, and bastions with gun-firing embrasures.

Namhansanseong is an excellent example showing the amplified use of natural barriers. The height of the mountain actually functions as part of the fortress, giving a great advantage to the occupants of the fortress. Staying focused in its objectives to be a defensive structure, even though the fortress is one of the largest in the country, there are no blind spots along the walls due to its curvature. Due to its collaboration with the natural features, even though it is a massive military structure, the scenery of Namhansanseong is very harmonious with nature. The fragment piling style walls, utilizing the topography of mountains, could save manpower and materials. Therefore, the period of construction was shorter and deployment of military forces was easy. Compared to the other huge mountain fortresses constructed to carry out defense on

Fortress Wall of the Lookout at 2nd South Outwork

Area near the Sueojangdae Post (West Command Post)

Tips for enjoying Namhansanseong

1. During the Joseon Dynasty, the Namhansanseong Emergency Palace was the only temporary palace that housed the shrines of the royal ancestors and the altars of the deities of earth and grain which signifies the important role as the emergency capital. Many cultural

events take place in the Namhansanseong Emergency Palace and tour guide programs in Korean, English and Japanese are available.

2. Sueojangdae Post (West Command Post), provides a grand vista to both inside and outside of the walls of Namhansanseong. The West gate lookout is a great location to appreciate the geographical relation between Namhansanseong and the capital city of Seoul.
3. Since the reign of King Injo, Namhansanseong was repeatedly repaired and reconstructed. It was continually managed by monk-soldiers of Military Buddhist Temples as well as regular soldiers from Suoecheong army corps headquarters. A visit to Janggyeongsa temple in the eastern area and the archaeological site of Hanheungsa temple recently excavated will provide an insight into the people who built and protected the fortress.
3. The development of fortress construction can be clearly seen through the fortress walls and especially the 1st, 2nd and 3rd South Outworks.
4. Bongam and Hanbong extented defensive walls are preserved in their original form from when they were built during the reign of King Sukjong in the 17th century.

prolonged wars in the 17th century during the Joseon Dynasty, Namhansanseong is superior in its size and condition of preservation.

More Information

Namhansanseong Culture & Tourism Initiatives, The Guidebook of Namhansansenog's Historic documents for standard Interpretation of Heritage, 2012.

The Namhansanseong Studies Series Vol. 1, NCTI, 2011.

The Namhansanseong Studies Series Vol. 2, NCTI, 2011.

The Namhansanseong Studies Series Vol. 3, NCTI, 2012.

The Namhansanseong Studies Series Vol. 4, NCTI, 2013.

The Namhansanseong Studies Series Vol. 5, NCTI, 2014.

Namhansanseong(Nomination Dossier), Cultural Heritage Administration of Korea, 2013, Republic of Korea.

WHC-14/38.COM/8B, Nominations to the World Heritage List p. 30.

Historic Villages of Korea

Hahoe and Yangdong

Jeoung Myoung Sik (Cultural Heritage Administration)

Hahoe Village and Yangdong Village

The two historic villages are in Andong City and Gyeongju City of Gyeongsangbuk-do Province of Korea. Both are family clan villages established around the 14th~15th centuries and are exquisite reflections of the traditional Confucian philosophy. Clan villages were local communities formed by family members of the same surname. Together they cultivated the land, studied and lived together, and the villages consist of houses, pavilions, study halls, and Confucian academies.

Hahoe village is composed of the Ryu family, whilst Yangdong village is occupied by the families Yi and Son who are interconnected by marriage. Of all the World Heritage properties in Korea it is the only one with residents living inside the property. The location of the village and the layout of the

Andong Hahoe Village

houses in harmony with the natural environment fully respect the principles of pungsu (traditional geomancy principles). The two villages are representative examples of the typical village settlement in Korea, one by the river and one on the foothills of a mountain. The Confucian lifestyle and traditional culture are still inherited up to this day.

Hahoe Village

Hahoe Village is perceived like a landscape painting when one reaches the top of Buyongdae Cliff and looks down at the village. The name Hahoe (河回, meaning meandering water) is derived from the natural setting of the Nakdonggang River flowing in an S-shape around the village. The Ryu family members live around the main road in the center of the village, whilst other surnamed families live in the outskirts of the village.

The village is preserved in its original layout. The architectural features showing the living culture of Joseon such as Yangjindang House, Chunghyodang House, Bukchondaek

Hahoe Byeolsingut Mask Dance

House and Byeongsanseowon Confucian academy all stand intact boasting their traditional beauty. Thatch-roof houses encircle the large yangban tile roof houses showing the features of a yangban village.

Coexistence of the folk culture and Confucian culture

Hahoe Village stands out from other traditional villages because the Confucian culture was preserved together with the village as well as the surrounding natural environment blending in with the human settlements.

The Hahoe Byeolsingut Mask Dance is closely related to the beliefs of the villagers. It started around the mid-12th century wishing for the peace and prosperity of the village. Made famous because of its masks, the dance also included satirical banter of the commoners mocking the yangban class and society. It is one of the representative community folk entertainments which is handed down together with the Seonyu Julbul Nori (Boat ride and fireworks). It is interesting to note that at a time when Confucianism was at its peak, folk culture such as the mask dance also prospered in the village of Hahoe.

A village cultivated by the Pungsan Ryu Clan

Currently over 70% of approximately 100 households in Hahoe are Ryus who descend from the same ancestry. In

Byeongsan Seowon Confucian Academy

Dongwonrok, a document produced in 1642, it records that most of the villagers are Ryus with a few Heo and An family members living in the village. Ever since the 17th century Hahoe was raised by the Ryus. Ryu Jonghye, the first member to settle

Seowon, Confucian Academies

As private educational institutions during the Joseon Dynasty, Seowon had two functions. One was to educate Confucian scholars and the other was to enshrine renowned and famous scholars of the past. Children from yangban families would stay in these academies to study and to conduct ritual services to the ancestors. These academies were the center of regional scholars and families, influencing the local politics.

The most representative head house of Hahoe Village is Yangjindang. As a yangban household of the Joseon Dynasty it is the oldest building in the village.

Across the road from Yangjindang stands Chunghyodang, the head house for the descendants of Ryu Seongryong. It was erected after the death of Ryu Seongryong by his descendants and students.

Wonjijeongsa Study Hall

Bukchondaek House

in Hahoe started the clan village and Seoae Ryu Seongryong[1] is the most representative historical figure of the family.

Ryu Seongryong and Byeongsan Seowon Confucian Academy

Ryu Seongryong (penname Seoae, 1542~1607) is a representative figure of Hahoe Village. He was the Prime Minister of Joseon during the Seven Years War against Japan, who was also an exceptional scholar and official who appointed General Yi Sunsin and Gwon Yul to overcome the crisis of war.

His intellectual compositions include Jingbirok and Seoaejip, which document and study the Seven Years War. His spiritual tablets are housed in Jondeoksa Shrine inside Byeongsan Seowon Confucian Academy, approximately 3km away from Hahoe Village. Byeongsan Seowon is recognized for its distinguished architectural features, and the landscape view from Mandaeru Pavilion looking out to the Nakdonggang River is counted as one of the best views of Korea.

The Story of Yangdong Village

The Yeogang Yi clan was the first to settle in this village, and members of the Pungdeok Ryu clan married into the daughter of the Yi family and settled together. Later on the Gyeongju Son

1) Ryu Seongryong is a civil official from the mid-Joseon Dynasty. He was Commander-in-Chief during the Seven Years War against Japan who had the insight to appoint Yi Sunsin and Gwon Yul as generals of the Korean navy and army to overcome the national crisis.

clan married into the daughter of the Ryu family and prospered together in the village. Yangdong Village soon became the community for the Yi family and the Son family. To settle near the relations of the wife was a common practice in early Joseon and both the Yi and Son families still live together in Yangdong.

The tile-roof houses of the yangban (noblemen) are located in the higher grounds whilst the thatch-roof houses of the commoners surround the yangban houses from below. The village shows a typical yangban village layout.

View of Yangdong Village

The village sits amidst the four valley ranges of a mountain and together with the stream flowing by the side the overall

Gyeongju Yangdong Village

Marriage Customs of Joseon

Settling in with the wife's family meant that the man would join his wife in her hometown and follow the customs of his in-laws. An expression for getting married (gyeolhonhada in Korean, gyoelhon meaning marriage and hada meaning to do) was to phrase it as 'going to the wife's in-laws house' janggagada. Jangga means the house of the wife and gada means to go. In this custom the husband moves into his wife's house and lives there for a while. This was a representative marriage custom until the mid-Joseon Dynasty.

However as Confucianism became deeply rooted as the dominant doctrine, the customs changed into having the wife joining the husband's house and the expression for getting married changed into sijibgada (sijib meaning the house of the husband and gada meaning to go). Until now, both expressions janggagada and sijibgada are considered as equivalent phrases for getting married.

village is shaped like the Chinese character 勿 (mul). The village naturally formed on this spot taking into account the conditions for auspicious sites according to pungsu principles and the surroundings also ensure the security of the village. On the highest grounds tile-roof houses were built and commoners houses were established alongside the small roads interconnected to the main roads. The thatch-roof houses nearby the yangban houses were usually occupied by commoners or servants. The family ancestral shrine housing the spiritual tablets of the forefathers are located at the rear and innermost spot of the yangban households. In quiet locations of the village there are Confucian academies and village schools for education and studying. Also at secluded spots with beautiful scenery, there are pavilions and study halls which were used by the scholars of the village. As such the purpose and usage of each space was separated.

Representative Architecture of Yangdong

Hyangdan has a unique layout resembling the character 興 (heung), with the men's quarters, women's quarters and the servants' quarters centering around the courtyard. The house was endowed by King Jungjong to Hoejae Yi Eonjeok, a renowned Confucian scholar when he was looking after his sick mother during his post as governor of Gyeongsang Province.

Gwangajeong was the house of Son Jungdon who served as the Minister of Interior in the mid-Joseon Dynasty. It is located around the middle of the western most hill of the village overlooking the agricultural fields in front. The name of the house means 'to watch the children grow as the grains grow in the fields'.

Seobaekdang is the head house of the Wolsong Son family.

Thatch-roof houses of Yangdong Village

Mucheomdang is the detached house of the scholar Yi Eonjeok. It is a representative yang-ban household being both stylish yet austere. The plaque reading 左海琴書 (Jwahaegeum-seo) written by the Prince Regent Daewongun, father of King Gojong still hangs on top of the wooden floor.

Diary of a Carpenter

It was in 1996 as a student studying architecture that I became acquainted with the two villages. It was a ten-hour round trip from my home in Gwangju, but every holiday was filled with study visits to the two villages together with my colleagues, as they were essential places to visit when studying traditional houses and villages of Korea. 15 years later, I became the head carpenter of the 'Conservation Team for State-designated Heritage' and was responsible for the conservation and management of the two villages in preparation for the field evaluation of UNESCO. It was my dearest hope that the two villages with such long tradition and history could be inscribed on the World Heritage List, so that they could be better protected in the future. The wish came true in 2010 when it was decided at the World Heritage Committee meeting to inscribe the two villages. The day of inscription is still memorable when I shared the happiness together with the villagers. The outstanding conformity of the traditional buildings and the surrounding environment are wonderful cases presenting the society and culture of the Joseon Dynasty. Now the two villages of Hahoe and Yangdong are heritage to be cherished by humanity.

* Note : Guided tours are available in Yangdong Village at 10, 11, 13, 14, 15, and 16 o'clock. Guides are provided in Korean, English, Japanese and Chinese.

More Information

Doosan Encyclopedia

Inventory of Cultural Heritage, Cultural Heritage Administration, 2010

Stories of Korean Architecture, Kim Bongryol, Dolbegae

UNESCO World Heritage, Korean National Commission for UNESCO Website http://www.unesco.or.kr/heritage/

UNESCO World Heritage from School Textbooks, Lee Hyungjun, Sigong Junior, 2011.

Military architecture of the 18th century

Hwaseong Fortress in Suwon

Lee Ji Eun (Seoul National Univ.)

A city made by the determination of one man, Hwaseong

Hwaseong Fortress running 5.7km sits in Suwon city in the middle of Gyeonggi-do Province. One had to pass through Suwon in order to reach the capital city Hanyang from the southern regions of Korea such as Jeolla-do and Chungcheong-do Provinces. One of the three main roads connecting the capital city to the southern local regions passed through Suwon. Suwon functioned as an important crosspoint during the Joseon Dynasty.

Although Joseon was a Confucian country, the 18th century slowly brought on changes to the society. The agricultural basis became diversified with the increase of mercantile activities, which also triggered the growth of cities. Many people gathered to the capital Hanyang in search of new technologies and

Hwaseomun Gate and the Northwest Gongsimdon (Obeservation Tower)

information. The scholars pursuing the School of Practical Learning also dreamed of building a new Joseon.

Jeongjo, the man who yearned for a strong Joseon

Jeongjo was crowned the 22nd king of Joseon in 1776. As soon as he became king, he moved his father's tomb, Crown Prince Sado (or Posthumous King Jangjo) to Suwon and named the tomb Hyeollyungwon. He also planned to build a new city nearby his father's tomb with the function of protecting Hyeollyungwon. His endearment towards his late father disguised his true motive which was to yearn for a "world of new order" reinstating strong royal authority. He wished to promote commercial and business activities in his new city of Hwaseong, and also wanted to benefit the people of Joseon by developing new agricultural techniques.

In other words, building Hwaseong did not merely mean that new fortress walls and new office buildings were built to create a new city, but it was an innovative attempt to manifest the new ideas from the School of Practical Learning. Starting with land compensation to the residents of the Hwaseong area, the Suwoncheon Stream was reinforced as infrastructure to the new city, and new roads were laid down. The project did not end with building Hwaseong Fortress, but continued on to ensure the livelihood of the city by establishing a maintenance

Building method of the fortress as suggested by Jeong Yakyong

Jeong conjectured that the walls bulging out in the middle was the cause for the easy collapse of existing fortress walls. Therefore he suggested a new method of building up walls for Hwaseong Fortress. It was to build up each row of stone slightly inching inwards up to 2/3 of the height of walls, and then to push the stones outwards slightly with each row to the top. He also suggested 0.9cm for the difference between each layer. Even today the upper middle part of Hwaseong Fortress appears to be slightly protruding out.

and development office, and setting up Manseokgeo, a large reservoir nearby to ensure the increase of resident income and to promote commercial activities.

The men who created Hwaseong

The person who played the most important role in building Hwaseong was Dasan Jeong Yakyong. Entrusted with Jeongjo's confidence after his success in planning for the Baedari Bridge crossing the River Hangang, Jeong studied fortress architecture of China and read various science and technology books of the Western world acquired via China. On the basis of his studies, he papered a document called "Seongseol (城說, The Definition of Fortress)" in the winter of 1792. In this paper, he planned

Fortress walls of Hwaseong

Why does the Janganmun Gate protrude out?

Janganmun Gate was originally supposed to be built slightly inwards, towards Paldalmun Gate of the south. On 15th January 1794, King Jeongjo went up Mount Paldalsan to view the potential site of Janganmun Gate. The site was marked with a flag amongst the commoners houses. The king asked, "Is that not a village?" An accompanying official answered, "Yes sir it is. We are planning to demolish those houses in order to build Janganmun in that spot." Hearing that the king replied, "It appears that it would cause many houses to be pushed outside the fortress walls. If they are all demolished it would be in contrary to my words of prizing the unity with my people. Build Janganmun Gate to the outside of all the houses."

This is the reason why the fortress walls coming from Hwaseomun Gate protrude out before they reach Janganmun Gate.

the overall size, material and architectural method of Suwon Hwaseong Fortress, and it was by this plan that the fortress was built.

The other hidden contributor to the construction of Hwaseong Fortress was Jo Simtae. He was a military official, head of the naval forces of the three southern regions, who was responsible for moving the Suwon Magistrate's Office whilst constructing Hyeollyungwon Tomb. He was the chief officer on-site responsible for the construction of Hwaseong Fortress. As the person in charge of the entire construction and management of documenting the protocol records, he can be likened to the

Hwahongmun Gate, the northern water gate of Hwaseong Fortress

modern day Project Manager.

Construction methods and business management concept of 200 years ago

The construction of Hwaseong Fortress started on 7th January 1794 by collecting stone, despite the worries of many officials.[1] Initially 10 years was estimated for the entire construction, however with the completion ceremony taking place on 16th October 1796, the whole process merely took 2 years and 10 months.

1) 『Hwaseong Seongyeok Uigwe Amended Korean Translation』 2001, Gyeonggi Cultural Foundation, p12

Such efficiency in shortening the construction time was made possible due to the focused task management of King Jeongjo and with the utilization of efficient technology. A temporary agency responsible for the construction of Hwaseong called 'Seongyeokso' was established and 2,188 officers and craftsmen worked for the agency.

Modern engineering technologies were applied to the entire construction. Jeong Yakyong invented a new machine called the geojunggi and yuhyeonggeo based on the principles of the pulley imported from the West, which dramatically shortened the entire process. Stone materials were procured through private businesses, by determining the needed size of the

Seoammun Gate (West Secret Gate)

Responsible official names inscribed on the fortress walls on Changryongmun Gate

stones (large, medium, small, rubbles) and ordering only the necessary amount. The stones were delivered cut readily so that they could be used in the construction immediately. Also in order to heighten the sense of responsibility of the engineers to enhance the solidity of the structure, all names of the officials and artisans involved in the construction work were inscribed on the fortress walls near the gates.

Modern day management concepts can also be seen in the construction of Hwaseong Fortress. King Jeongjo was gifted with the ability of managing human resources which he thoroughly displayed in the construction of Hwaseong. Compared to other national construction works where the labor of the people were drafted without compensation, the construction process of Hwaseong stands out as the people involved were paid wages on a half-day basis. Artisans were grouped into three categories and those who excelled and proved to be productive were merited. The common people participating in the labor were provided with fur hats, emergency medicine (*jejungdan*) and heat prevention medicine (*cheokseodan*). Fur hats at that time were luxury items and symbol of high status only available to upper class officials above the 3rd rank. The display of the King's regard for the people boosted the motivation of the workers and contributed in raising the quality of the construction.

The building of Hwaseong Fortress was made possible with King Jeongjo's vision for a new world order and the dedication of his officials.

View of the Hwaseong Temporary Palace

Janganmun Gate

Hwaseong Fortress steps up to the world

In April 1997 Hwaseong received an important guest. Professor Nimal De Silva, an architect and heritage expert from Sri Lanka visited Hwaseong to conduct the field evaluation for the World Heritage inscription of Hwaseong. In fact the original walls and buildings of Hwaseong Fortress built in the 18th century had been nearly demolished through the Japanese Colonial Period and the Korean War, and the existing standing structure was restored in the 1970s. Professor De Silva had doubts about the authenticity of the fortress as eligible for World Heritage.

However when historian Yi Jonghak handed him the *Hwaseong Seongyeok Uigwe* (Royal Protocol on the Construction of Hwaseong Fortress), he was astounded and convinced by the meticulous records and the thorough restoration conducted adhering to the written records. At the 21st session of the World Heritage Committee, Hwaseong Fortress was inscribed on the World Heritage List as a representation of the pinnacle of 18th century military architecture, incorporating the best scientific ideas from Europe and East Asia brought together.

The 'Royal Protocol on the Construction of Hwaseong Fortress' which played an important role in ensuring the World Heritage inscription is a full record of the entire construction process, giving deep insight into the architecture, culture, arts and science of Joseon. As part of the entire collection of the

Construction records from the Royal Protocols on the Construction of Hwaseong Fortress

In the section of Janganmun Gate, details such as the number of nails and exact points of usage are meticulously recorded.

Nails of 2-ja 5-chi 12 (used for the angle rafters)

Nails of 1-ja 236 (used for the nurigae, sara, yongdu and tosubagi)

9-chi Flat headed Nails 660 (used for the jamsang and basis for convex tiles)

*ja, chi are traditional units of measurements

Sinpungru Pavilion of Hwaseong Temporary Palace

Tips for enjoying Hwaseong Fortress

1. The 24 skills of martial arts are performed in front of the Hwaseong Temporary Palace inside the fortress. It is based on the comprehensive martial arts book "Muyedobotongji" compiled by Baek Dongsu, Yi Deokmu and Bak Jega upon the orders of King Jeongjo. It is a great chance to experience the essence of the Joseon Dynasty military training.
2. Take the chance to approach the fortress walls and check if the suggestions of Jeong Yakyong in building the fortress walls were actually adopted.
3. The roof of Banghwasuryujeong Pavilion is shaped like a cross which is a rare case to be found in Korea. A similar example can be found only in Buyongjeong Pavilion inside Changdeokgung Palace.

4. The night view of Hwaseong Fortress is not to be missed. The beauty of Korean fortress architecture can also be appreciated at night as it opens to the public in the evenings.

Royal Protocols of the Joseon Dynasty, the records themselves have been inscribed on the UNESCO Memory of the World Register in 2007. It is a rare example of an architectural feature and its accompanying records both being recognized in global lists.

More Information

Hwaseong Seongyeok Uigwe Amended Korean Translation, Kim Manil et al., Gyeonggi Cultural Foundation, 2001

Studies on the Management of Hwaseong by King Jeongjo, Choi Hongkyu, Iljisa, 2005

Suwon Hwaseong, a new city of Joseon built on the ideas of Practical Learning, Kim Dongguk, Dolbege, 2002

Jeongjo Yi San erecting Hwaseong, the city of his dreams, Kim Junhyeok, Yeoyudang, 2008

The establishment of Hwaseong by Jeongjo, Choi Hongkyu, Iljisa, 2001

Timeline of the World and Korean History at a glance

Years	Korean History	World History
~ BCE 1000	700,000 years ago, Paleolithic Age BCE 8,000 Neolithic Age BCE 3000~2000 Gochang, Hwasun and Ganghwa Dolmens constructed BCE 2333 Dangun establishes Gojoseon Kingdom and places the capital city in Asadal BCE 2000 Development of the Bronze Age culture and Gojoseon	BCE 3500 Start of the Mesopotamia Civilization BCE 3000 Start of the Egyptian Civilization BCE 2500 Start of the Indus, Huanghe Civilizations BCE 1500 Start of the Shang Dynasty in China Rise of the Hittites BCE 1200 Trojan War
BCE 999~	BCE 450 Buyeo Kingdom established Jinguk established BCE 400 Spread of Iron Age culture BCE 194 Wiman crowned as King of Gojoseon BCE 108 Fall of Gojoseon	BCE 770 Spring and Autumn Periods in China BCE 753 Establishment of the Roman Empire BCE 525 Unification of the Orient by Persia BCE 334 Conquest of Alexander the Great BCE 322 Unification of Northern India by the Maurya Dynasty BCE 264 Punic Wars (~146) BCE 221 Unification of China by the Qin Dynasty BCE 202 Establishment of the Han Dynasty in China
	BCE 57 Silla established BCE 57~CE 935 Gyeongju Historic Areas BCE 37 Goguryeo established BCE 18~CE 660 Baekje Historic Areas BCE 18 Baekje established	
CE 1~400	3 Goguryeo relocates capital to Guonei City 42 King Suro establishes Garakguk Kingdom 53 King Taejo crowned in Goguryeo 234 King Goi crowned in Baekje 244 Wei Dynasty attacks Goguryeo 313 Goguryeo defeats Lelang Commandery forces	25 Start of the Eastern Han Dynasty in China (~220) 45 Start of the Kushan Empire in India 96 Era of the Five Good Emperors in Rome (~180) 226 Start of the Sassanian Empire in Persia 280 Unification of China by Western Jin Dynasty

Years	Korean History	World History
CE 1~400	256 King Naemul crowned as King of Silla 372 Goguryeo accepts Buddhism 384 Baekje accepts Buddhism	313 Edict of Milan 320 Establishment of the Gupta Empire in India 375 Migration Period in Europe 395 Split of the Roman Empire into East and West
401 ~ 600	472 Goguryeo relocates capital to Pyong-yang 43 Silla-Baekje Alliance breaks down 475 Baekje relocates capital to Ungjin 494 Goguryeo annexes Buyeo Kingdom 572 Silla officially recognizes Buddhism 552 Baekje spreads Buddhism to Japan	439 Start of the Northern and Southern Dynasties in China 476 Fall of the Western Roman Empire 486 Start of the Francia Kingdom 520 India, Decline of the Gupta Empire 589 China Unification by the Sui Dynasty (~618)
601 ~ 800	660 Fall of Baekje BCE 18~CE 660 Baekje Historic Areas 668 Fall of Goguryeo 676 Silla unifies the Three Kingdoms 689 Balhae established 774 Establishment of Seokguram Grotto and Bulguksa Temple	610 Start of Islam 618 China, Start of the Tang Dynasty (~907) 687 Reign of Pepin II, Frankish Kingdom 750 Start of the Abbasid Dynasty (~1258) 800 Charlemagne crowned Emperor
801 ~ 1000	900 Gyeonhwon establishes Late Baekje (Hubaekje) 901 Gungye establishes Late Goguryeo (Hugoguryeo) 918 Wang Geon establishes Goryeo 926 Fall of Balhae 935 Fall of Silla BCE 57~ CE935 Gyeongju Historic Areas 936 Goryeo unifies the Late Three Kingdoms	829 Establishment of the Kingdom of England 843 Treaty of Verdun 907 Fall of Tang, Start of the Five Dynasties (~960) 907 Start of the Liao Dynasty (~1126) 960 China, Start of the Song Dynasty (Northern Song,~1127) 962 Otto I establishes the Holy Roman Empire (~1806) 987 Start of the House of Capets in France (~1328)
1000	1033 Construction of Cheollijangseong Fortress (~1044)	1000 Invention of the compass and gunpowder in Song Dynasty

Years	Korean History	World History
1000	1086 Uicheon publishes Sokjanggyeong Buddhist scriptures	1037 Establishment of the Seljuq Turk Empire (~1157) 1086 Campaign of the Crusades (~1270)
1100	1107 Yun Gwan conquests Nuzhen tribes 1145 Kim Busik compiles the Chronicles of the Three Kingdoms 1170 Military Coup d'etat	1115 Start of the Jurchen Jin Dynasty (~1234) 1127 Fall of Northern Song, Start of Southern Song Dynasty (~1276) 1192 Start of the Kamakura Shogunate
1200	1219 Opening of Mongol relations 1231 First Mongol Invasions 1234 Sangjeonggogeumyemun published with metal type prints 1236 Goryeo creates Palman Daejang-gyeong woodblocks 1274 First Japanese Expedition of Goryeo and Yuan Forces 1290 Acceptance of Confucianism	1206 Unification of Mongolia by Genghis Khan (~1368) 1215 Issuance of the Magna Carta, England 1271 Establishment of the Yuan Dynasty (~1368) 1279 Fall of Southern Song, Unification of China by Yuan 1299 Formation of the Ottoman Empire (~1922)
1300	1304 Daeseongjeon Shrine established in National Academy 1359 Invasion of the Red Turbans 1376 Choe Yeong conquers the Japanese pirates 1377 Choe Museon establishes Office for Gunpowder Jikji Simche Yojeol printed 1388 Wihwado Retreat 1389 Bak Wi subjugates Tsushima Island 1392 Fall of Goryeo, Start of Joseon 1392~1945 Royal Tombs of the Joseon Dynasty 1394 Capital city placed in Hanyang 1394 Establishment of Jongmyo Shrine	1302 Establishment of the Estates General in France 1337 Start of the Muromachi Shogunate in Japan 1337 Hundred Years' War between England and France (~1453) 1368 Fall of the Yuan Dynasty and rise of the Ming Dynasty (~1644) 1369 Establishment of the Timurid Dynasty (~1500) 1378 Western Schism of the Church (~1417)
1400	1405 Construction of Changdeokgung Palace Complex 1443 Hunminjeongeum, the Korea alphabet created 1457 Haeinsa Janggyeong Panjeon rebuilt	1414 Council of Constance (~1418) 1455 Wars of the Roses in England (~1485) 1467 Start of the Sengoku Period in Japan 1492 Columbus arrival in the American Continent

Years	Korean History	World History
1500	1592 Japanese Invasion of 1592 (Seven Years War against Japan)	1517 Protestant Reformation initiated by Martin Luther 1536 Protestant Reformation initiated by John Calvin 1543 Copernicus presents heliocentrism 1590 Unification of Japan by Toyotomi Hideyoshi
1600	1600~ Hahoe and Yangdong Villages 1636 Manchu Invasion of 1636 1678 Casting of Sangpyeongtongbo Coin	1600 Establishment of the East India Company in England 1603 Start of the Edo Shogunate in Japan 1616 China, Start of the Qing Dynasty 1642 Start of the English Civil War
1700	1712 Erection of Baekdusan Mountain National Boundary Monument 1796 Construction of Hwaseong Fortress in Suwon	1776 US Declaration of Independence 1789 French Revolution
1800	1831 Catholic Church establishes the Joseon parish 1871 US expeditions to Korea in 1871 1882 Treaty of Peace, Commerce and Navigation between Korea and US endorsed 1883 Taegeukgi used as Korean national flag 1895 Eulmi Assasination of Queen Myeongseong 1392~1945 Royal Tombs of the Joseon Dynasty 1897 Establishment of Daehan Empire	1804 Coronation of Napoleon as Emperor 1861 American Civil War (~1865) 1894 Sino-Japanese War 1896 First Games of the Modern Olympics
1900	1904 Korea Japan Protocol endorsed 1907 Abdication of Emperor Gojong 1909 Japan signs Gando Convention with Qing China An Junggeun assasinates Ito Hirubumu	1902 Signing of the Anglo-Japanese Alliance 1904 Russo-Japanese War (~1905)

Years	Korean History	World History
	1910 Loss of national sovereignty	
1900	1919 Korea Republic Provisional Government established 1945 8 · 15 Liberation 1948 Establishment of the Government of the Republic of Korea 1950 Korean War	1907 Formation of the Triple Entente 1914 World War I (~1918) 1939 World War II (~1945) 1945 Establishment of the United Nations 1995 Establishment of the World Trade Organization
2000	2000 First Inter-Korea Summit Talks	

Author Introduction

Nam Chang Geun

Majored in traditional architecture at Cheongju University and worked as a researcher at the National Research Institute of Cultural Heritage in the Architectural Heritage Division. He became interested in restoring architectural remains dating from the Three Kingdoms Period to Goryeo Dynasty and had the chance to participate in the Joint North-South Manwoldae Excavation Project in 2007. During the 120 days he spent in Kaesong together with North Korean academics, he had the chance to understand their lives and also the chance to widen his understanding of the cultural heritage in Kaesong. He obtained his doctoral degree on the Architectural Characteristics and Restoration based on Remains of Gyeongryeong-jeon(Sanctuary) in Goryeo Royal Palace, based on his experience of the excavation.

From 2012 he is responsible for the Conservation project of Kaesong traditional houses' at the Gyeonggi Cultural Foundation. The traditional houses cluster area in the center of Kaesong constitutes the buffer zone of the Kaesong Historic Monuments and Sites which is a World Heritage property, being an important heritage protected by the government of North Korea. He hopes his works contribute to the cooperation and exchange between the two Koreas with a positive outlook on the future unification.

Baek Gil Nam

He majored in history education and Baekje history at Yonsei University, and Archives Management at the Korean Graduate School of Archival Science atMyongji University. He got interested inBaekje history while preparing for a field trip, which prompted him to continue his studies in graduate school, although at that time the history of Goguryeo gained a lot of attention due to the Northeast Project of the Chinese Academy of Social Sciences.

After the graduation, he lived diligently complying to the hardships of securing employment with just a history major. He worked at the Korean Institute for Curriculum and Evaluation during daytime, and went to graduate school of education at night. He studied archives management on weekends and had a part-time job at the Children's Museum of the National Museum of Korea. Working hard to keep food on the table broadened his areas of interest and deepened his academic insights.

Whilst working as a short-term teacher at a high school, he passed the curatorial examination and started to work at the Seongnam City Government. He is now responsible for the exhibition works at the HanseongBaekje Museum in Seoul. He imagines that someday people will picture Baekje when being asked a question about Seoul. He is interested in the political system and city structure of Baekje, and plans to study museum history education in the future.

Sim Joon Yong

He majored in History atYonsei University, obtained his Master's in

Archaeology atSejong University, and is now pursuing his doctoral degree in Architectural History at Myongji University. It was his hobby to gain as much work experience as possible as a student and hc went through more than 20 part-time jobs such as a roasted sweet potato seller, playing small parts in films, working at a movers, at the delivery service of a department store, as on-site staff at public events, and a waiter at a restaurant, including the running of a jazz bar. He found the field he wished to dedicate his life in, whilst working part-time at the university museum. He worked at the WonjuYonsei University Museum, Hangang Cultural Heritage Institute, whilst studying archaeology and participating in excavations. He also worked as a curator at the Paju City and Goyang City government whilst he studied traditional architecture. He left the civic office in pursuit of a more diverse field, and eventually established the A&A Culture Institute. He is now immersed in the fun works of museum planning, special exhibition consulting, writing project reports on cultural heritage, heritage utilization projects, and lectures on cultural heritage.

He is author of 『From Bukhansan of the Guinness Book to World Heritage, Royal Tombs of the Joseon Dynasty』, 『A Hundred Q&As for History and Culture of Gyeonggi Province』 (co-author), 『Visiting Gyeonggi Province with a Curator - Remains of Colonial Resistance』 (co-author), and 『Neolithic Culture of Namhangang River Area』.He has also participated in various heritage research projects such as 『Field study and research for developing activation strategy of social enterprise in cultural heritage』, 『Research on basic planning and suggestion of a operational model of Confucian Schools and Seowon』, 『Research on promoting community support projects in historic city conservation areas』. He dreams about achieving systematic conservation of cultural heritage and efficient utilization under the harmonious cooperation between private and public, academic researchers and site managers.

Lee Jun Sung

He entered theCollege of Humanities, Yonsei University, dreaming to become a journalist finding justice within society. However he became more attracted to the prudence of history and continued his study of ancient Korean history.

After his Master's degree, he completed his military service by teaching Korean history to cadets at the ROK Army Third Military Academy, at thedepartment of military history. It was during this time that he became interested in the protection of cultural properties within military camps, including the Goguryeo bastions. He is currently pursuing his doctor's degree on the state structure and political system of Goguryeo, and is a lecturer at Yonsei University and the National Traffic University of Korea.

Lee Ji Eun

She worked at an international firm dealing with semiconductor equipment for 10 years, and fearlessly jumped into the field of cultural heritage conservation to do what she 'really wanted to do'. She learned how to look at historic cities from the views of historic cultural environment at theUrban Planning Department of Kyungwon University and met many good people while she worked hard. Her master's thesis is about cultural heritage preservation in the view of project management inside historic cultural environment, and is now doing her doctor degree in environmental planning at Seoul National University. Now she is a much happier person than before.

Lee Hyun Sung

He dreamed of being an architect after he saw the Osaka Castle when he was in elementary school.After majoring in architecture at Seoul National University of Science and Technology, his interest in cultural properties started while working at the architecture history research center at Seoul National University. His master's thesis at Myongji University is about problems of cultural heritage restoration, and has been through various field experience at repair sites of cultural heritage.

He is currently doing his doctorate in Architectural History at Myongji University, feeling a need for more experience, and works at A&A Culture Institute as a team leader and works on consulting for the utilization of cultural heritage.

Jeoung Myoung Sik

His career as a carpenter for traditional houses started while he was studying architecture in university. From 2009 he worked as the team leader of the 'National Cultural Heritage Restoration Team', which examines and repairsthe 153 state-designated traditional houses and historic villages. Since 2011 he works at the Cultural Heritage Administration, and became a master carpenter, responsible for the management and repair of Changdeokgung

Palace and the five palaces, Jongmyo Shrine, and the Royal Tombs of the Joseon Dynasty. All three are inscribed on the World Heritage List. He is a lecturer for the 'Methodology of restoration and causes of deterioration in traditional houses' in the 『Training Course of Intermediary Manager of Korean Traditional House Construction』, operated by the Ministry of Land, Infrastructure and Transport from 2013. He regularly writes 'Story of Korean Houses' for the children's newspaper of Gangseo-gu.

Cho Doo Won

Cho Doo Won

Graduated from Department of Architecture and Engineering at Kyung Hee University, and completed his military services as a Reserve Officer. Initiated by a prize award at a design contest while he was a student, he became interested in studying architectural design for cultural heritage and continued his studies and works in Germany. He studied design and architectural conservation theory at the Aachen Technical University for his master's, and architecture conservation at the Bamberg University for his doctor's degree. He is responsible for World Heritage projects at the Namhansanseong World Heritage Center of the Gyeonggi Cultural Foundation from 2010. He is an active member of ICOMOS-Korea and as the Voting Member of ICOFORT. He has been the technical evaluator and desk reviewer for World Heritage nominations, and the evaluator for projects of the World Monument Fund.

Jo Eugene

She lived alternately in Korea and abroad during her childhood, and majored in Korean history at Korea University. After graduation, she worked at the Cultural Heritage Administration for 10 years on UNESCO related projectsand international exchange. Her main field of work has been on the nomination and management of World Heritage. She participated in World Heritage Committee meetings,5 times as part of a Committee State Party delegation and twice as a member state delegation since 2006. She was Rapporteur of the 18th World Heritage General Assembly in 2011, and has been nominated as Rapporteur of the 40th session of the World Heritage Committee in 2016.

She finished her master's at Hannam University with her thesis on the World Heritage Convention, and has continued her studies by enrolling in a doctorate course at Konkuk University on World Heritage. She has participated in the World Heritage nomination and inscription projects ofJeju Volcanic Island and Lava Tubes, Royal Tombs of the Joseon Dynasty, Historic Villages of Korea; Hahoe and Yangdong, Namhansanseong Fortress, and Baekje Historic Areas. She also continuously translates articles and texts related to cultural heritage into English.